Richard Mooney was born in Slough, England, and educated locally until the age of fourteen when schooling ended abruptly because of the war. He then travelled extensively in the Far East, learning Japanese at the same time. He is currently living in Kendal, Westmorland.

In this astonishing book, Richard E. Mooney develops his hypothesis first put forward in his immensely successful work, *Colony: Earth*, and brings new evidence to support it from biology, geology, archaeology and the myths and legends of mankind. His material ranges from the religious beliefs of Polynesian Islanders and Red Indians to photographs taken by Lunar Orbiter 2 of the Sea of Tranquillity; from experiments with cosmic rays in the Pyramid of Khephren to ancient texts detailing a knowledge of medicine and surgery equal to our own.

Gods of Air and Darkness is both compulsive and essential reading for all those whose curiosity about man's origins is strong enough to carry them into speculations beyond the narrow confines of traditional belief.

Also by Richard E. Mooney

Colony: Earth

Richard E. Mooney

Gods of Air and Darkness

The possibility of a nuclear war in the past

A PANTHER BOOK

GRANADA
London Toronto Sydney New York

Published by Granada Publishing Limited in 1977
Reprinted 1980

ISBN 0 586 04345 4

First published by Souvenir Press Ltd 1975
Copyright © Richard E. Mooney 1975

Granada Publishing Limited
Frogmore, St Albans, Herts AL2 2NF
and
3 Upper James Street, London W1R 4BP
866 United Nations Plaza, New York, NY 10017, USA
117 York Street, Sydney, NSW 2000, Australia
100 Skyway Avenue, Rexdale, Ontario, M9W 3A6, Canada
PO Box 84165, Greenside, 2034 Johannesburg, South Africa
61 Beach Road, Auckland, New Zealand

Made and printed in Great Britain by
Richard Clay (The Chaucer Press) Ltd
Bungay, Suffolk
Set in Linotype Times

For Mary

Contents

Introduction

This work is a sequel to *Colony: Earth* in which we attempted to show, primarily, three things:

1. That it is possible that Man neither evolved, nor was divinely created, but arrived here as a colonist from worlds elsewhere in space;

2. That the civilisation he created was destroyed in a vast catastrophe, which passed into legend as the 'Deluge' or 'Flood' and was followed by a memory of a time of Gods and a Golden Age;

3. That this catastrophe was responsible for the great extinction of life at the end of what we call the Pleistocene and gave rise to the Ice Age Theory. We suggested that the Ice Age was not in the PAST, but rather in the PRESENT.

It was hoped that these ideas explained many mysteries in the past: the lack of fossil evidence for evolution, the extermination of the mammoth and other species of animals of the Pleistocene, the existence of areas of knowledge in the past which does not fit with the concept of Mankind emerging for the *first* time from a state of barbarism – in particular we offered an explanation for the building of many structures, such as Stonehenge and the Pyramids for which no completely believable explanations had been forthcoming.

Obviously, a subject of this scope had, of necessity, to deal with some matters only briefly, and others scarcely at all. This present book, therefore, is an expansion on some themes, and presents new material stemming in part from discoveries made since the first book was written. No doubt a similar thing will happen to this book: by the time it is written, further new discoveries will have been made and new evidence made available which will either support the concepts in this book, or nullify parts or even all of it. This is a risk we shall have to take: So far, new discoveries made since *Colony: Earth* was written have tended to support the ideas contained therein, rather than detracted from them. It is to be hoped that this trend will continue.

In many ways, this volume will be more difficult to write than the previous book. In that, we dealt to a large extent with physical evidence, whereas in this volume the emphasis will be placed more on intangibles. With respect to many of the ideas we are seeking to elaborate, evidence is almost entirely missing. Thousands of archaeological sites which may yield valuable information and throw light on many mysteries have been investigated only scantily or not at all. Traces of vanished cities have been discovered in Death Valley in California and elsewhere in the Southwestern states of North America. Odd artifacts have been discovered, usually quite accidentally, throughout North America where the existence of a former high civilisation has never been suspected. No thorough archaeological investigation has been carried out at Tiahuanacu in Bolivia, and there are thousands of ancient sites throughout Central and South America awaiting investigation. The great number of stone circles and other megalithic alignments scattered throughout Britain and Western Europe have been almost ignored, many have been destroyed, and it is due almost entirely to the efforts of one man (Prof. A. Thom) that anything at all is known of these. Of course, there are exceptions. Stonehenge, Avebury and Silbury Hill have been carefully preserved as monuments from a former era. Measurements have recently been made at the great megalithic alignment complex at Carnac in France. But it may be many years before a systematic survey and mapping project of all the megalithic sites is undertaken. Only then may we discover if there was a link between them, or a plan of a coordinated mathematical scheme, possibly of great precision and importance, which may give us a clue to some of the mysteries of the pre-historic past. No one knows what may be hidden far beneath the great artificial hills of Avebury and Silbury, or beneath some of the lesser-known pyramids of Egypt, many of which are covered in sand and half ruined.

With each year that passes, our chances of solving the

mysteries of our past grow less: Time and the elements corrode and rot away the traces, and the bulldozers of our impatient age obliterate or cover up what may be evidence of primary importance. Most major finds of the most unusual kind have been made by pure chance: Galt's Cube, that strange steel object found inside a piece of coal, was an accident, as was the bell-shaped jar found encased in stone. Iron nails have been found inside stone, as was the trace of a screw. Parts of ancient batteries were found covered in dust in the corner of a Baghdad museum, labelled as religious bric-à-brac. Chance may uncover something sensational tomorrow, or we may discover nothing new for years.

In some areas of our investigation we have almost no signposts to show us the way. We shall have to try to analyse mythology in new ways: numberless books have been written on the ancient civilisations and their mythologies but beyond a certain point the experts are baffled. It may be that as long as we look at things in the traditional way, we will never understand, and never find the answers.

What is the underlying significance of all the world's religions, why do they all follow the same pattern, and whence came all our varied gods of the past? Why did they appear to have come into existence at a certain point in time and at no other? Why have not primitive peoples today created new religions like the old?

Why is there always, at the back of men's minds, the thought that there used to be a Golden Age on Earth? What is the true significance behind many of our deep subconscious images, such as the Great Sacred Egg? or the sensation, experienced in dreams, of levitation? Why do many people experience strange happenings in the mind – telepathy, precognition? Are there powers of the mind which are real, but hidden, lying dormant?

Flying saucers are not new: reports of them exist as far back as written records go. The first is mentioned on a papyrus in the reign of the Pharaoh Thutmosis III, 4,000 years ago, and many references in the biblical Old Testament can be equated with UFO reports. Are UFOs real, and if so, what are they?

All ancient religions speak of a great disaster in the past

and a disaster to come. In Eastern religions, World Ages are mentioned, cyclic destructions; and the Aztecs in the New World, like their neighbours, the Maya, were obsessed with the idea of future destructions. Has this significance, and if so, what could it be?

All these things, and more, we shall examine in this book, and try to fit into a logical framework. Many newer writers are searching for new answers to old mysteries. Daniken suggests that the Gods were astronauts from other worlds. Kolosimo suggests a similar approach, but with the additional emphasis on the concept of older advanced terrestrial civilisations. Tomas, in his examination of ancient scientific knowledge in his book *We Are Not The First*, considers the possibility of ancient societies possessing the knowledge we have today. These ideas are not particularly new. Professor Soddy, in 1909, discussed the possibility of a vanished culture with advanced knowledge, and Donelly's Atlantis and Churchward's Mu contain the concept of vanished, legendary empires. At the present time, these ideas are being taken more seriously, as older ideas and explanations fail to satisfy. However, even the newer concepts seem still to be inhibited by more traditional views, and thus fail to explain many of the phenomena they are confronted with. So they tend to introduce factors which are semi-mystical in nature, falling back on the idea of secret societies of ancient knowledge, or the unreal approach to the Atlantis problem made by Madame Blavatsky and the Theosophists. These fringe ideas threaten to bring into disrepute any serious attempt to take a fresh look at the ancient world, and have the unfortunate effect of lumping the serious, logical investigator with the rest of the 'lunatic fringe'.

In this volume, we shall try to avoid anything which seems mystical or magical. We shall extrapolate from facts and evidence, and interpret religion and mythology in the light of modern scientific discoveries. No matter how bizarre our extrapolations may seem, they are not beyond the bounds of the *possibilities* inherent in our present scientific knowledge or theories.

It has been said that introductions should properly belong at the end of a book, and not the beginning, and indeed, that some introductions are so long and so technical that it is almost superfluous to read the book!

On this note, therefore, we will end this introduction, and in the chapters that follow, the reader is warned that the facts are, as far as can be ascertained, *facts*, and the inferences drawn from them are the author's, to be taken seriously, or not, as the reader wishes.

1

Life and Intelligence

We do not know how life began on Earth, nor the how and why of the beginnings of the reasoning creature called Homo Sapiens – literally Wise Man. We also do not know whether or not life exists on other worlds in the Universe. Possibly we shall not know that until we are able to travel to those other distant worlds in space, and then perhaps we shall also find a clue to our own origins.

At the present time, most reasoning men believe in Evolution, the idea postulated by Charles Darwin that life had evolved over many ages, changing to fit differing environments and altering itself the better to survive. Darwin's theories have been modified somewhat in the light of discoveries made since his monumental *Origin of Species* was published, but basically, the concepts of 'Evolution by Natural Selection' and 'Survival of the Fittest' are the keys to modern thought on the origin and development of life. There are others who believe in a Divine Act of Creation, and even those who believe in Evolution feel that behind the workings of life's ceaseless change and growth is a master mind, a Supreme Creator.

There are those who are unable to believe either in a transition from the inorganic to the organic in the misty past of Earth's beginnings, or in Divine Creation, and who seek answers elsewhere. Alternatively then, we have the Panspermia Hypothesis, first postulated by Svente Arhennius in the seventeenth century, by which means spores, or seeds of life, drifted from the reaches of space and came to life on the Sun-warmed surface of the Earth. A later variant on this idea was that perhaps these spores had drifted, dormant, across interstellar space from distant stars, or that accidentally, or perhaps deliberately, life had been seeded here by a spaceship from another world which had visited in the distant past.

Divine Creation and Evolution both suggest a strictly terrestrial origin, which has led to the assumption that there is something special about the Earth as the place where life developed. In recent years it has been suggested that where Evolution is concerned, this pattern could be repeated on many worlds where the conditions are suitable for its development, and alternative biochemistries have been suggested for planets which do not meet the requirements for the development of terrestrial forms of life. On the other hand, Divine Creation generally assumes that the Earth was picked specially by the Creator as the only abode of life in the Universe. This gives the Earth special meaning to which it scarcely seems entitled when it is considered that the planetary system to which this world belongs does not occupy any particularly significant place in the Galaxy, and is probably one of many millions of planetary systems.

The Panspermia Hypothesis in its original form postulated that spores would be driven by light pressure towards a planetary body, and this would mean that they would be driven outward from the Sun. For spores to have reached the Earth, therefore, they would have had to come from nearer the Sun or the inner planets, and it is doubtful whether such spores would have survived the high temperatures prevailing in this region.

For spores to have reached the Earth from the neighbourhood of other stars, it is only conceivable that they could have been carried here either accidentally or deliberately by an object of artificial origin entering this Solar System.

The first traces of life reckoned to be a blue-green alga which has been dated at 2,500 million years old. However, what is more certain is that life appeared suddenly to manifest its traces in the Palaeozoic Period some 600 million years ago, with the different phyla (families) of early molluscs, fishes, insects and plants already separate and developed. The stages which had led up to these divisions cannot be traced. It seems certain that plant life gained a hold on the land surfaces before life eventually emerged from the seas, and this is easy to understand. Until the plants had converted the primitive atmosphere to an oxidising one by releasing oxygen into the atmosphere, animal life would have had to remain aquatic and draw its oxygen from the water. Only after sufficient oxygen had been released would animal life be able to survive on the land.

It is curious that the Book of Genesis specifically mentions this *order* of creation, viz:

Genesis 1. v.9. 'And God said, "Let the waters under the heaven be gathered together into one place, and let the dry land appear." And it was so. God called the dry land Earth, and the waters that were gathered together he called Seas. And God saw that it was good. And God said, "Let the Earth put forth vegetation, plants yielding seed, and fruit trees bearing fruit in which is their seed, each according to its kind, upon the Earth." '

v.20. 'And God said, "Let the waters bring forth swarms of living creatures, and let birds fly above the Earth across the firmament of the heavens." '

v.24. 'And God said, "Let the Earth bring forth living creatures according to their kind; cattle and creeping things and beasts of the Earth according to their kinds." '

Surely it was not by chance that the chroniclers of old had the sequence ordered correctly. It seems more likely that they had drawn on knowledge of the correct sequence, knowledge of the same kind that we have acquired.

It is somewhat vague, admittedly; we do not have a wealth of detail – there is no mention of what kind of *beasts* emerged, and in what order. No mention of the early amphibians, or the great reptilian order of dinosaurs who lorded the Earth during the long period of the Mesozoic.

Here, we have a great unresolved mystery. We have divided up the past into three great epochs – the Palaeozoic, the period of primitive life and the early amphibia; the Mesozoic, the age of the great reptiles; and the Cenozoic, when the reptiles were replaced by the mammals. But no one knows why the dinosaurs died out and were replaced by mammals. Many theories have been advanced for their decline: fluctuations in temperature, to which the dinosaurs, presumably being cold-blooded, were unable to adjust; or the gradual desiccation of the swamps in which they are presumed largely to have lived; or radiation from a nearby nova. We simply do not know, and all the answers to the problem which have been suggested so far are a long way from being satisfactory.

We cannot be sure even that the dinosaurs *were* cold-blooded creatures like modern reptiles, and some of which do live in temperate climates with cold winters, through which they hibernate. Further, it has been found that the dinosaurs lived on every continent and in every part of the world. Their bones have been found in England and Europe, America, Asia, India, the Gobi Desert, the tundra of the present Arctic lands and even Antarctica. It would appear that the whole planet was warm from pole to pole, and there is no evidence to suggest that the entire planet became cold, or even partially glaciated during the Mesozoic.

More recent research on skeletons of the Brontosaurus, the largest of all the dinosaurs, has tended to reverse the earlier opinion that this was a swamp-dwelling creature. It had been thought that because of its great bulk and weight, the creature must have spent the greater part of its life in swamps, where the water could easily support its weight without placing too great a strain on its limbs, while its long neck would enable it to feed on vegetation from the floor of the swamp. Further examination of the limb structure, together with footprints outlined in solidified soils, have led to a theory being developed that the Brontosaurus' mode of life actually resembled that of a modern elephant or a giraffe. Its heavy, columnar legs were straight, rather than bent, and its foot was shaped similarly to that of the elephant. The conclusion has been drawn that the Brontosaurus lived on open or semi-open plains, and used its long neck to live off the tops of trees in the way that the elephant uses its trunk or the giraffe its long neck. It is possible that others of the great dinosaurs had a similar environmental adaptation, and that the flesh-eating dinosaurs such as Tyrannosaurus Rex preyed on the more harmless vegetable-eaters: a situation similar, in fact, to that obtaining on the plains of East Africa today, where there are long dry seasons and alternate rainy seasons. If this were so during the Mesozoic, then periods of desiccation would scarcely have led to the extinction of the dinosaurs.

The suggestion that radiation from a nearby nova, or perhaps an outburst of excessive radiation from the Sun, put an end to the age of the dinosaurs is also fraught with difficulties, the main one being that if the dinosaurs were killed by excessive radiation, then all forms of life would have been similarly affected, including the small mammals who existed at the time, and the Earth today would be barren.

Furthermore, why was it that only the dinosaurs, of all the kinds of life existing at the time, died out? There were also the first birds, the early mammals, and many forms of fish, molluscs and amphibians in the sea, and multitudinous varieties of insect life, many of which have remained apparently scarcely changed since Palaeozoic times.

Also, not all the dinosaurs are extinct, as there is one species, the Tuotara, which lives in New Zealand, and has remained apparently unchanged since Mesozoic times, with an ancestry directly linked to the reptilian orders of that era. Of course, this is only a small reptile – many of the species of dinosaur of Mesozoic times were quite small, one being as small as a mouse – and confined to this one area only, with perhaps the island's isolation being a factor in its survival.

An exceedingly primitive fish, the coelacanth, was supposed to have become extinct many millions of years ago, but more than one of these creatures have been caught in recent years, which is further proof that not all the species from remote times are no longer alive, and there may still be others to be discovered.

It does seem, however, that it is not factors of climate, excessive heat or cold, or radiation, which were responsible for the death of the reptiles of the Mesozoic, as there is little doubt that they would be capable of surviving comfortably in our warmer climatic zones. There must be another answer to what appears to be a selective death of many ancient species.

Could it be that the great saurians did not die naturally, but were killed off deliberately? This would mean an intelligently directed policy of destruction, presumably undertaken by human beings. The objection would be immediately raised that human beings were not in existence contemporary with the dinosaurs, which died out some sixty million years ago, when Homo Sapiens only appeared, according to our anthropologists, 35,000 years ago.

Are we sure, however? We do not know how long mankind has been on the Earth, although the general opinion is that True Man, Homo Sapiens, has not been here for more than 30,000 or 40,000 years in his present form. There are, nevertheless, some peculiarities; consider ...

A shoeprint was discovered in a seam of coal in Fisher Canyon, Nevada, and the impression of the sole was so clear that the strong thread was visible. This print is estimated to be fifteen million years old.

Dr Chow Ming Chen, in the Gobi Desert in 1959, found the impression of a ribbed sole on sandstone, reckoned to be millions of years old. Dinosaur footprints have been found in similar sandstone beds.

A rock carving in the American south-west, at Hava Supai Canyon, Arizona, shows a Mesozoic Brontosaurus. A rock drawing, also from North America, shows a clearly recognisable Stegosaurus, also a Mesozoic Saurian.

A design on pottery discovered at an ancient site at Cocle, in Panama, bears a striking resemblance to a Pterodactyl, also stemming from the Age of Reptiles.

Shoeprints, drawings of dinosaurs – the artifacts of man – which could be contemporary with the dinosaurs. What are we to make of this? Were the drawings made from life, on the spot? Was someone walking around in shoes at the same time as the dinosaurs were living on the Earth?

Either Mankind was living here at the same time as the dinosaurs – 100 million years ago – or the dinosaurs did not live as long ago as we have thought. Perhaps our dating is all wrong. Or perhaps Man was not living here at this remote period, but was visiting this world by spacecraft from other planets. Were there, perhaps, visitors from a highly advanced civilisation elsewhere in space who came here and deliberately killed off the dinosaurs? We have not been able to explain satisfactorily that the dinosaurs died off naturally. In that case, was their extermination deliberate? Either Man was living here at this time, and killed off the dinosaurs, or he visited from elsewhere for the same purpose.

If Man was living here at this remote period, then it is understandable that he destroyed the great reptiles, as they would constitute a great menace, particularly the large carnivorous varieties, and even the vegetarians would consume an enormous quantity of vegetable foodstuffs useful to Man. If, however, he was a visitor from elsewhere in the Universe, why go to such trouble? It would only be perfectly understandable if this world had been selected for colonisation by civilised people from elsewhere in space. Under these circumstances it would be logical to eliminate any large and possibly dangerous forms of life.

This point of view may mean that Mankind, if not already living here, was visiting this planet many millions of years ago, if our dating of dinosaur bones is correct. In this connection, it is interesting to note the unusual finds of artifacts which could date from Mesozoic or even earlier. There is the example of Galt's Cube, a steel cube found in a bed of coal in Silesia, and which must have got there before the coal bed was formed. This would place the object in Carboniferous times, many millions of years earlier than the Mesozoic. There is the further example of a bell-shaped jar found inside rock, which could also be many millions of years old. It is not beyond the bounds of possibility, therefore, that spaceships from other civilisations have been visiting this planet over a period of hundreds of millions of years.

We are faced with another problem when considering the extinction of the dinosaurs, and that is sudden transition from one pattern of life to another. The end of the supremacy of the great saurians ushered in the age of the mammals, and it has been suggested that with the end of the dinosaurs, the small mammalian forms which were living at the time could then expand and fill the ecological niches left by their disappearance. This answer, too, is vaguely unsatisfactory.

As we have already stated, the first appearance of life on Earth was a blue-green alga some 2,500 million years ago. Suggestions have been made that there may have been earlier and even more primitive unicellular forms preceding this, perhaps 3,500 or even 4,000 million years ago, which would make it possible that life appeared soon after the Earth was formed. We have also seen that clearly recognisable fossils commence abruptly some 600 million years ago with the major phyla apparently established, and with no intermediary stages.

As the *Scientific American* of August 1964 says:

'Both the sudden appearance and the remarkable composition of the animal life characteristic of Cambrian times are sometimes explained away or overlooked by biologists. Yet recent palaeontological research has made this sudden proliferation of living organisms increasingly difficult for anyone to evade ...

'These animals were neither primitive nor generalised in anatomy; they were complex organisms that clearly belonged to the various distinct phyla, or major groups of animals, now classified as metazoan. In fact, they are now known to include representatives of nearly every major phylum that possessed skeletal structures capable of fossilisation ...

'Yet before the Lower Cambrian there is scarcely a trace of them. The appearance of the Lower Cambrian fauna can reasonably be called a "sudden" event.

'One can no longer dismiss this event by assuming that all pre-Cambrian rocks have been too greatly altered by time to allow the fossils ancestral to the Cambrian metazoans to be preserved ... even if all the pre-Cambrian ancestors of the Cambrian metazoans were similarly soft bodied and therefore rarely preserved, far more abundant traces of their activities should have been found in the pre-Cambrian strata than has proved to be the case. Neither can the general failure to find pre-Cambrian animal fossils be charged to any lack of trying.'

We observe a further point in a book, *Synthetic Speciation*, by Dr Heribert Nilsson, Professor of Botany from the University of Lund, Sweden.

'If we look at the peculiar main groups of the fossil flora, it is quite striking that at definite intervals of geological time they are all at once and quite suddenly there, and moreover, in full bloom in all their manifold forms. And it is quite as surprising that after a time which is to be measured not only in millions, but in tens of millions of years, they disappear equally suddenly. Furthermore, at the end of their existence they do not change into forms which are transitional towards the main types of the next period; such are entirely lacking.'

The same thing which holds true of plant life, also holds true for animal life on Earth. Entire groups hold sway for many millions of years, abruptly disappear, and are suddenly replaced by other forms completely different.

This factor is one of the main stumbling blocks to a complete acceptance of the evolutionary theory, which is today being increasingly questioned. It is known that all forms of life, whether they be plant, insect or animal, are basically composed of elements which are common in the universe. Oxygen, hydrogen, iron, copper, calcium, which are some of the elements which make up living forms, are common in the composition of stars and planets, and even in interstellar dust and gas. What makes the great difference between organic and inorganic is their *organisation*. There is another factor to be taken into account, *something* which defies the inorganic world's tendency to simplification, to breaking down into constituent elements, and replaces it instead with an ability to grow and replicate. It is this argument, now being revived in some circles, that there may be another form of energy, a 'life force', which somewhat strengthens the hand of the adherents of Divine Creation against the Evolutionists.

A hypothesis to be proposed here admittedly does not solve the problem of how life may have arisen in the *first* instance in the Universe, which is something we may never know; and it will be said that placing the *origin* of life as a whole on some hypothetical planet perhaps many millions of light years away is dodging the issue. So it is, but so also is Divine Creation, and the stubborn insistence on the veracity of an unproven theory of evolution.

What we are merely attempting to do is to advance an alternative suggestion to the other two, in view of the present evidence.

Let us therefore follow up the suggestion that this planet may have been visited by intelligent life from other worlds in the remote past. Could some of these visits have taken place *before* there was any life here at all? Perhaps this Solar System was surveyed soon after its formation – thousands of millions of years ago – when it was observed that at least one planet (Earth) was at the correct orbital distance from the primary to support a carbon-based life form. Two other planets (Mars and Venus), and possibly at this time, a further planet also fall within this category, within what the astronomers term the 'life-zone', with perhaps the Earth as first choice.

Our hypothetical spaceship lands and its crew begin the task of seeding the ground with the vegetation which will commence the process of converting the atmosphere from a reducing one to an oxidising one. A selection of animal forms are introduced into the warm, chemically rich seas. The starship, its task completed for the time being, leaves for home. Perhaps monitoring devices are left behind, to register the progress of the early experiments. In the course of time, when the level of oxygen in the atmosphere has reached a certain level, further forms of life are deposited – those capable of living on the land surface. Larger and more advanced forms are introduced from time to time. We have to assume that this process would take perhaps millions of years, and we are of course unable to imagine a race which could create a civilisation stable throughout the millions of years which would be needed to undertake such a task. So possibly such projects are undertaken by several races, and there exists in some Superior Galactic Civilisation a Central information pool, a great computer complex, for example, whereby information is listed on potentially habitable systems where such projects have been initiated, and thus made available to any race capable of using the information. It must be realised that a certain planet, the Earth for instance, will not always be habitable for Man, as stars have a finite lifetime and the planets which surround them live or die at the dictate of the primary. The giver of life is also the bringer, eventually, of death. There must be millions of planets in this Galaxy alone which have been, are now, or will be at some time in the future habitable for creatures such as Man; and it may have been that Homo Sapiens originally arose on a world not only millions of light years away, but millions of years ago in time. If the human race came here as migrants at some time in the past, it may be that they had to forsake a world no longer habitable, or that they were sent here to inhabit a planet made suitable for the race. One can visualise humanity endlessly moving from planet to planet, as older ones die and new worlds are born, a continuous restless star-travelling to ensure the continuity of the race. Possibly this process has gone on for countless millions of years, and will do so for millions of years to come. Eventually, of course, it will be necessary to evacuate a large number of this world's inhabitants, perhaps to the planets of other stars, and it may even become necessary in the distant future to modify those other planets to make them suitable for human occupation – a concept already under serious consideration by our space scientists, and known as planetary engineering. It may also be possible to alter human beings by processes of advanced biological engineering to adapt them to different environments to those we are used to. If we take the concept that Man may be a migrant to this planet at some time in the past as reasonable and logical, then it would explain certain things which have been given other explanations. For example, Man suffers from an extremely painful spinal affliction known in common parlance as 'slipped discs', allegedly caused by stress. This condition has been explained by some biologists as due to the fact that as descendants of quadrupedal animals, we are not yet used to walking upright, and that too great a strain is placed on the spinal column in what virtually amounts to an unnatural stance. It could also be, of course, that we are not yet fully adapted to the heavier gravity field of this rather massive planet, particularly if the ancestral home had either been a planet with a lesser gravity; or the race had been spaceborne for a long period and used to a lesser artificial gravity. The fact that the gravitational pull of the Earth makes some activities difficult and arduous – climbing and lifting weights – may also point to the fact that we are not yet fully adapted. This could also lead us to suspect that as we are not yet fully adapted, we have not been here for too long a period of time.

If then, at a remote period, the Earth had been prepared for later human colonisation, it is difficult to reconcile this with the existence of dinosaurs which had to be eliminated to allow for the settlement of human beings. Perhaps they were an experiment which went wrong – they grew too large, or multiplied too rapidly; or perhaps for some reason or other the Earth was left, forgotten, for millions of years. Perhaps the alien biologists were conducting a long-term test with various forms of life under conditions which at that time may not have been suitable for humans, when the Sun was much younger.

At any rate, eventually the dinosaurs were replaced by mammalian forms, and a balanced ecological cycle created suitable for human colonisation, which followed at a later stage.

Admittedly, it may sound like fantasy, but in some respects it *does* fit the evidence we have available, and it is not a project which is utterly impossible.

Consider – we have life, organised in distinct groups, which appear suddenly and as suddenly and mysteriously vanish, to be replaced by other forms, fully developed, which bear no relation to the previous groups. We can say the same thing in respect of Mankind, as, in spite of the vast amount of research which has been undertaken, no links have been proven between certain anthropoids and true human beings. Mankind appeared as suddenly as the other species and as fully formed.

Many mythologies tell of a God (in the case of the Hebrews), or of gods, who created all life on Earth. It is perhaps significant that these mythologies tell of experiments and errors which were made by the gods, whereby some of the forms of life they created had to be destroyed. These could be oblique references to the disappearance of forms of life now extinct, such as the dinosaurs. The pattern of life which has been followed – the step by step sequence which our biologists tell us is the only logical one, and which is supported by religious literature – would seem to have had an intelligent direction behind it. It was

neither random nor haphazard. Of course, this is true of
the whole of creation, as, naturally, a random or haphazard system would be unworkable, so an orderly pattern
would be necessary even if the whole system of the Universe was somehow spontaneous and self-creating.

But – what if this story of the gods creating life were
true? Were they really gods, or have they come down to us
in a distorted form? Perhaps the deity who created life on
Earth was in reality a man, or rather, a team of people –
biologists, ecologists, mathematicians. Perhaps there is a
hint of this in Genesis where God says: 'And let us make
Man in our image.' Why the plural, if there is only one
omnipresent God? In fact, we come across this plurality on
several occasions. There are the Sons of God who mate
with the women of Earth and produce remarkable children.
Does this perhaps relate to visits by astronauts at later
times and who had children by the descendants of the
earlier colonists? One God who created all the Universe
surely would not have children. It has been explained by
some experts that the Sons of God was merely a title given
to a certain group (perhaps a religious group such as the
Essenes), but such people would hardly have produced
extraordinary children 'as the mighty men of old' as it
says in Genesis. It would also appear that this part of the
Genesis mythos stems from an extremely remote period, to
judge from its lack of detail.

In Isaiah, it is stated that God was coming in his great
anger to destroy the whole land, and that he came with a
mighty host and the weapons of his indignation. Once
again, the hint is that God was not singular, but one of
many.

We could look at this problem from the other end of the
scale, and imagine that Man has reached one of the inner
planets, say Venus or Mars. Neither of these worlds, if
Earth-like conditions prevailed, would be uninhabitable to
people from Earth.

If, at some later date, men reach Mars and find that soil
conditions are not too hostile, it may be possible to plant
extremely hardy alpine type plants – high altitude grasses
from the Andes or the Himalayas. If they flourished, and in

sufficient quantities, they would, in the course of time through the action of photosynthesis, have the effect of releasing oxygen into the Martian atmosphere. A denser oxygenated atmosphere would mean that the planet would retain more solar heat and the planetary temperatures would rise. At a later stage, lower altitude plants could be spread, and eventually a stage would be reached where plants, including trees, could be introduced from temperate or warm terrestrial zones. Once this was accomplished, animals, birds and insects could be introduced, and a balanced ecology of flora and fauna would eventually be reached. We would now have reached the stage, after a long period of time, when colonists could be introduced to a planet which now more closely resembled Earth. The atmosphere may still be thinner than on Earth, and the average temperature much cooler – Mars is 141 million miles from the Sun compared to Earth's 93 million miles. Perhaps the first colonists could be people used to high altitude conditions – Indians from the Andes or Himalayas, together with Europeans adapted to high altitudes and cold climates. Later still, settlers from lower altitudes and warmer climates would find little difficulty adapting to their new world. These colonists would build cities and transportation systems, farm the land, undertake forestry and mining, and manufacture all their requirements, in short they would do everything that we do today on Earth. Many generations would pass, those born on the planet would be perfectly adapted to the prevailing conditions. It is also true that such people, born on another planet, would have difficulty surviving on Earth, as the gravity on Mars is only a third of Earth's. They would therefore find the gravity of this planet an insupportably crushing weight. Being born in a lighter gravitational field would produce adaptive differences: they would be perhaps much lighter and taller in build than their earthly ancestors, and although more delicate-looking than their cousins from Earth, on Mars they would be capable of the same physical feats as Earth-bound people.

If we imagine, for some reason, communication was lost between the planets in the course of time, and that this lack of contact was continuous over a period of many thousands of years, and if we further consider that it is possible that future generations of Earth-descended Martians may forget their true origins, then a peculiar situation arises.

They may suffer setbacks in their world: disastrous wars, bringing a temporary return to barbaric conditions. The ships that brought them would long before have been broken up and their materials used for other purposes, or they may have been returned to Earth. After many thousands of years, new religions may spring up, and new mythologies be created about their origins.

Eventually, they could reach the stage we have now reached. If they had forgotten their true origins, their researchers would be faced with the puzzle as to where life had sprung from so suddenly and without preliminary stages. They would be able to say quite confidently that the first stage was vegetation, followed by various kinds of animals, birds and insects, all in their distinct groups, but would be unable to say how they had evolved there, as the preliminary stages leading to such evolution would be missing. They would be in the same difficult situation regarding the Martian people. Their anthropologists would seek in vain for the primitive stages which led to the present advanced Martian humanity, and perhaps propose an evolutionary theory even though the main proofs for such a theory were entirely lacking.

Their theologians and philosophers would also have to endeavour to unravel a curious mythology stemming from their very earliest days, as their true origins may not have been entirely forgotten, but preserved in a very garbled form. Perhaps they had legends about the time when gods came down out of the sky and brought life to a dead world, and when this was done, they also put people there, to multiply and flourish. Perhaps there would be a legend about the first people – or were they Gods? – who travelled across a great darkness to their new world, and had a recollection of another world which could be seen from the Martian sky.

How much of these legends would be believed by the hard-headed latter-day Martian savants? No doubt they –

being 'realists' – would scorn these legends as fairy stories from the infancy of the Martian race, stories of a fanciful explanation of how everything got there. Yet, this mythology would actually be the truth of how everything happened, and they would look in vain for a native Martian origin.

I believe we today are in the same position as those hypothetical latter-day Martians. The circumstances they would find *are the same as we find ourselves in today.*

The foregoing is just not science-fiction fantasy. We have already seen that such planetary engineering may one day be a possibility for our race. Seeding the carbon-dioxide clouds of Venus with bacteria to assist in the converting of the atmosphere to an oxidising one is being given serious consideration by our scientists, as is the possibility that we may be able to give life to the planet we have just mentioned by the methods we have outlined.

Of course, these are extremely long-term projects, and it is doubtful if they could be undertaken in our present economic or political climate; but we may be driven to these actions by harsh necessity in the years to come, perhaps by circumstances external to the Earth, or, more likely, by pressures which will be created here by over-population, the scarcity of various raw materials and fuels, or the dangers of a nuclear holocaust.

It seems now that we ought to see if there is any justification for the concept that we may have descended from voyagers from other stars in the distant past, and are, in fact, a race whose ancestors were not terrestrial Man, but Galactic Man. There are certain elements in mythology which are possibly clues which could lead to this assumption. The fact alone of the existence of such myths should make us ponder.

2

Humanity – A Spatial Origin?

Mankind evolved from a remote, apelike ancestor whom we cannot exactly trace, and who died out after giving birth to Homo Sapiens. This, briefly, is what the anthropologists tell us. Mankind lived in a very primitive state as a hunter and collector of berries and roots for many thousands of years, perhaps even tens of thousands of years, before he 'accidentally' managed to grow some grains and thus commence the first settled agricultural communities, which led eventually to cities and civilisation. This is what the pre-historian tells us.

If everything was so simple and straightforward, why are we confronted with so many puzzles about our past? Why are there such huge and all-important gaps in the evidence? Why do we have such curious mythologies? If Man had always been primitive and gradually fought his way from a savage state to civilisation, this should be reflected in our mythology and legends and in the folklore of the human race. Especially in view of the time factor. According to the pre-historians, it is only a matter of some 8,000 years ago since the first settled agricultural communities came into being. Written records of at least *some* kind are known to extend back to roughly 5000 BC; so there is a gap of perhaps two thousand years from the first settled agricultural communities and the invention of writing and records. We can assume that by the time village communities with their early farming techniques came into being, they would have to devise some means of keeping records of their flocks and herds, particularly on ownership. This alone would be an incentive to creating some form of written language – perhaps a primitive picture writing. Tallies made on stone and bone showing phases of the Moon, which may perhaps be calendric computations, have been found and dated by scientists to an extremely ancient period, perhaps even tens of thousands of years ago. So if people in the remote past were able to do this, it is just as likely – and far more useful on a practical level – that they kept some form of records of their possessions. Yet none survive from the earliest agricultural period. What is more, several thousand years is not a great period of historical time, and if one counts two generations to a century, information could be passed twice a century, or twenty times in a thousand years. We have indeed evidence of tribal traditions and oral mythologies passed down for periods of thousands of years. Many South American peoples and island Polynesians have remarkably detailed Flood legends, passed down orally, which must be many thousands of years old, as this event must have taken place prior to 4000 BC. So traditions of Man's emergence from a savage state to civilisation, which one would think should be a matter of pride for any human group, should be widespread throughout world mythologies. In fact, there are not even scattered references to the theme. On the contrary, in fact, most legends of the origin of Man depict an early paradise and its loss through a great calamity for which the 'gods' must take a large share of the blame. The Biblical 'Fall of Man' story is a case in point.

We are thus confronted with an intractable problem where humanity is concerned. If Man had evolved from an apelike ancestor, and then lived for tens of thousands of years as a primitive, what forces triggered off the sudden emergence of highly advanced civilisations in the past? Further, it has been stated that the development of the human brain was so staggeringly rapid by evolutionary standards as to be almost instantaneous. Apparently, we have here a dilemma which the theoreticians are unable or unwilling to admit exists. Where the question of the Ice Age in the past is concerned, it has been frequently stated that 'no known natural forces which can be visualised can account for the glaciations or their sudden termination'. With Mankind we could say the same thing. No known *natural* forces could have shaped the human mind in such a short period of time, a period which can be measured not in hundreds of thousands, but in mere tens of thousands of years. The idea goes entirely contrary to the evolutionary concept of minute mutations building up into major alterations only over millions of years. Some biologists have thought that even if life as a whole has developed in an evolutionary manner, the period has been too short for human intelligence and reasoning to have developed naturally.

Yet the evolutionary anthropologists and biologists cling doggedly to their theories even when neither the evidence nor the pattern fit. One suspects that they are unable to believe in the miraculous and are reluctant to admit to any other kind of possibility.

In his book, *Return To The Stars*, Erich von Daniken is aware of this problem, and quotes Loren Eiseley as follows:

> Today on the other hand we must assume that man only emerged quite recently, because he appeared so explosively. We have every reason to believe that, without prejudice to the forces that must have shared in the training of the human brain, a stubborn and long drawn out battle for existence between several human groups could never have produced such high mental faculties as we find today among all peoples on the earth. Something else, some other educational factor, must have escaped the attention of the evolutionary theoreticians.

Daniken thus assumes a *physical* evolution to be possible although more likely induced by deliberate and planned genetic mutation; but he finds that the explosive radiation of *intelligence* must have been artificially produced. His theory is that highly advanced aliens from another civilisation in space, armed with a vast amount of biological knowledge, genetically altered existing human stocks to produce a high degree of intelligence. They biologically programmed specimens for higher intelligence, at the same time implanting in this intelligence certain basic knowledge necessary for the development of civilisation, as well as moral values and religious concepts. These religious concepts induced such awe of the 'heavenly gods' (the aliens) so that the programming could be effectively carried out and there would be no sliding back to an animal state. He states that the severe penalties instituted in many ancient communities for attempted mating with animals, for instance, were instituted by the alien 'gods' to prevent such degeneration.

This speculation offers a solution of sorts to the sudden emergence of human intelligence, but there are many objections to it, and some factors that are not taken into account.

For one thing, Man cannot mate even with those animals physically nearest to him – the anthropoid apes – *and produce offspring*, because each species carries within it a specific number of chromosomes: for example, the human being has twenty-three pairs (forty-six) and a bee sixteen. Only creatures with the same number of chromosomes can mate and produce offspring, which is why every separate species breeds true to type. Alone of earthly creatures the human being has forty-six chromosomes; so he cannot produce offspring with any other creature on Earth but another human being. The question of Mankind producing bestial offspring simply *cannot* arise.

Even fossils of extinct apelike forms do not show any characteristics which could confuse them with Homo Sapiens, which tends to confirm the fact that there could not have been any hybridisation between human stocks and anthropoids or any extinct pre-hominid types. Homo Sapiens not only appeared on the terrestrial scene extraordinarily abruptly, he also appeared apparently without any direct ancestors, and he remains radically different, both physically and mentally, from any other anthropoid, past or present. Alien biologists embarking on a programme of genetic engineering would have had to amend drastically Man's physical structure, as well as make radical genetic alteration to his brain.

It seems doubtful if any civilisation from a planet elsewhere in the Universe would go to such lengths to populate a planet with intelligent life, particularly if the life they intended to create was identical to their own. 'After our likeness, in our image,' says the Bible, which suggests that what our ancestors called the 'gods' were human in form, although the exact relationship between man and the gods is an open question.

Hypothetical aliens, furthermore, would be unlikely artificially to produce an intelligent race which might one day become a menace to them. Daniken's suggestion that certain knowledge was implanted genetically in the race, to be brought forth in stages, is open to this objection. He suggests that the invention of printing, the motor car, aircraft, etc., were neither accidents, nor the inspirations of gifted men, but part of a 'programme' implanted by alien intelligences. But would another race implant in men such dangerous ideas as space flight capability, coupled with the discovery of nuclear weapons and missiles? For if we are to assume that the 'inventions' of printing, medicine, etc., were the result of alien programming, we should also include our fearsome arsenal of weaponry, the concepts of concentration camps, total war, and racial hatred. And these are the creations of an advanced and benevolent civilisation!

It seems to me far simpler, and also far more likely, that any advanced space-travelling civilisation which discovered an Earth-type planet not inhabited by intelligent life, would colonise such a planet for their own use, by their own people. No doubt any civilisation that has reached a state of advancement sufficient for space travel will also have largely conquered illness and its own planetary environment, and thus come up against problems of overpopulation. Colonisation of other planets could thus become a necessity. It has certainly been our experience on Earth that the more we control our environment for the safety of humanity, the more humans there are that survive, and this leads to overpopulation and the straining of all resources. Eventually, if our civilisation survives and large-scale space travel becomes a viable prospect, the stage could be reached when colonisation of other worlds will become both desirable and necessary to us too.

In a previous work – *Colony: Earth* – the possibility was raised that Mankind may originally have been of extra-terrestrial origin, the descendants of colonists from other worlds. This concept would both explain the suddenness of the appearance of humanity, with so much knowledge already implanted, and also explain why there are three basic human groups – Negroid, Mongoloid and Caucasian. The evolutionary theory, Divine Creation, and the newer theories of creation by artificial mutation *all* fail to explain satisfactorily why there should be these differences. All human groups can interbreed, which shows that they belonged to a common stock *at some point in time*. It is also true that the physical differences have no special bearing on survival capabilities in this particular planetary environment. Caucasian and Mongol occupy similar temperature zones, and the Negroid appears to have no difficulty in adapting to colder climates than those natural to him. We have mentioned in Chapter One an idea that Man may have been a traveller in the Galaxy for millions of years, moving from planet to planet as circumstances changed, and that his original home may perhaps be many, many times removed from this Earth. Could it be perhaps each of the human groups made transitory homes on the planets of several *different* suns, with slightly different radiation emissions, so that there would have been variations in the adaptive make-up of each group over vast spans of time?

If we refer to our hypothetical Martian model in Chapter One, we note that as we may one day send people of differing physical characteristics to another planet, other civilisations may have done so in the past.

Can we find any justification for advancing a case for extra-terrestrial colonisation? Such an event should have left at least a trace in racial memory, or in primordial folklore. I think we can. Legends quoted by Daniken, for example, to support his theories of Gods from space, could in fact even better support the idea that it is Man himself who was originally the God from space.

Some of the Polynesian islanders have a curious mythology, which was recorded by Bengt Danielsson, a companion of Thor Heyerdahl on the Kon-Tiki Expedition. Danielsson notes a discourse of a priest called Te-Yho-e-te-Pange, on the island of Raroia in the Tuamotu group.

In the beginning, there was only empty space, neither darkness nor light, neither land nor sea, neither sun nor sky. Everything was a big silent void. Untold ages went by. Then the void began to move and turned into Po. Everything was still dark, very dark, then Po itself began to revolve. New strange forces were at work. The night was transformed.

The new matter was like sand, and sand became firm ground that grew upwards. Lastly, the earth mother revealed herself and spread abroad and became a great country.

There were plants, animals and fish in the water and they multiplied. The only thing that was lacking was man. Then Tangaroa created Tiki, who was the first ancestor.

Is this legend in fact a distorted description of a voyage through interstellar space until the Solar System, and then the Earth, is reached? A journey through space would be without day or night, land, sea or sky. The first day would only commence when the planet's surface was reached, and conditions that we consider normal were experienced. We observe in the legend that all plant and animal life was in existence on the world, *except Man*, and this, again, agrees with our science, which states than Man came last into the world.

There is an American Indian epic called Chon-oopa-sa ascribed to an Indian poet called Pa-la-ne-a-pa-pa, and mentioned by Churchward in connection with his Mu theories.

The extract quoted here is interesting:

> In the remotest past
> Millions and millions of moons ago
> The first of mortal men was cast down
> On this world by the great Wo-Kon.
> The first Dakota was formed from a star;
> He hurled him and watched him as he fell
> Through the darkness until he rested
> On soft soil. He was not wounded,
> Wa-kin-yan, the first Sioux.

Legends such as these are not unusual in North America. The Canadian journal *Topside* says: 'The writer has recently met Chief Mezzaluna of the Piute tribe. In answer to the question Where did the North American Indians come from? the following was stated: "According to our ancient traditions the Indians were created in the sky by Gitchie Manitou, the Great Spirit, who sent down here a big thunderbird to find a place for his children to live. He discovered this land ... and brought Indians to settle on it. They were taught to use the land wisely and never abuse its natural resources." '

On the other side of the world, the Soviet scholar Viaceslav Saitsev says in his book *On Earth and Sea*:

> According to a Slavonic tale 'man was created far from the Earth and very long ago. When God had finished creating He commanded the angels to take some human couples to Earth so that they should multiply there. The angels spread the couples over the world and wherever they set up home they multiplied. Perhaps when Earth is nearing its end, God will again take men somewhere else so that they may reproduce.' The mind which worked out such a tale must have been an elaborate one, fully developed. Though there may be fantasy here it is not without sense.

Clearly, we do have legends which connect Man's origins with a 'spatial' birth. The Polynesian description of space is scientifically accurate. The American Indian legend of the thunder-bird is interesting, as this is widespread throughout North America and could have a basis in fact. A thing which flies and makes a sound like thunder – this somewhat reminds us of a rocket, which does make a tremendous noise. Eskimos also have a legend that long ago they were brought to their present homeland by great iron birds, although this may not necessarily mean space flight.

The *Rigveda* is the most ancient of the Indian sacred Sanskrit texts. From Paul Frischauer's book *It Is Written* we quote the following:

In those days there was neither not-being nor being. Neither the atmosphere nor the sky was above. What flew to and from where? In whose keeping? What was the unfathomable? In those times there was neither death nor immortality. There was not a sign of day and night. This *one* breathed according to its own law without currents of air. Everything but this was not present. In the beginning darkness was hidden in darkness. The life-powerful that was enclosed by the void, the one, was born by the night of its hot urgency ...

Was there an above, was there a below? Who knows for sure, who can say whence they originated, whence this creation came?

An ancient prayer in the Egyptian Book of the Dead says:

> O world egg, hear me.
> I am Horus of millions of years
> I am lord and master of the throne.
> Freed from evil, I traverse the ages
> and spaces that are endless.

There is also the concept in ancient literature that the time standards of the 'gods from the sky' were different from those of mortals of Earth. For instance, a day of Brahma is equivalent to 4,320,000,000 years to a mortal. It is also said of God in the Bible that 'a thousand years in Thy sight are but a moment'.

What can we make of all these legends? Why should they exist? It may seem that they make very little sense unless we look at them within the context of *spatial travel and Einsteinian physics*.

First, we have accurate descriptions of outer space: darkness, neither day nor night, no air. How could our primitive ancestors have known of these things? Without even aircraft, how could they possibly have known that a point could be reached when there would be no atmosphere? A state of neither day nor night would also have been totally outside their experience. Knowledge must have been passed down to them in some manner, and in spite of some distortions, the descriptions are basically what long-distance space travellers would bring back with them. And it is certain that without *experience* of these things, it would not have been possible to have written about them so accurately. The unimaginable, that which is *totally* outside the terrestrial frame of reference, cannot be imagined, much less with accuracy.

The *Rigveda* makes a curious statement, when it says 'there was neither death nor immortality'. What can this mean? If it is not death or immortality, and presumably it does not refer to normal mortal life, then it means something else, and this something could have been suspension of faculty – suspended animation. Translated into modern scientific terms, the statement in the *Rigveda* could refer to a journey in space. 'Neither the atmosphere nor the sky was above' – were these space travellers in a state of suspended animation? 'This one breathed according to its own law without currents of air.' In a state of suspended animation as envisaged by our scientists for long-duration space flights, neither air, food or drink would be taken, as the suspended travellers would be enclosed in an air-tight capsule, with automatic life-support systems at a minimum setting. This is graphically described in the film *2001: A Space Odyssey*. The reference to one who breathed by his own law could perhaps be referring to such a state if obeying 'its own law' is seen as opposed to obeying the laws of earthly life. 'Living, but not breathing' could perhaps be a translation. Normal life would be resumed at the termination of the journey when the Earth was reached and the travellers were revived.

The reference in the Egyptian prayer seems to point to Horus being a space traveller. The curious statement that the gods who travelled in the voids of space lived at a different time-rate to mortals is not so curious if it is taken in the context of space travel undertaken at near relativistic velocities. At these speeds, the now well-known 'time dilation' effect is operative, whereby a journey lasting many light years to people on Earth, actually takes a much shorter period to those undertaking the journey.

A round trip to Alpha Centauri, for example, would take approximately ten years at near relativistic speeds (Alpha

Centauri is 4·3 light years distant from Earth). To the travellers, however, the voyage would appear to have taken only a matter of weeks. This is not to say that time *itself* is altered or slowed, but that the apparent distance is decreased and therefore does not take as long.

This factor could lead us to question whether in fact the space-travelling gods of antiquity in *actuality* were much longer-lived than Earth-bound people, or whether this was an effect of time dilation. An astronaut travelling from a distant solar system could make visits to Earth several times in his lifetime, whereas to the people on Earth the visits would be at intervals of hundreds of years. The fact that many generations of Earth-bound people would be born and die in the lifetime of the visiting astronaut could well give rise to the impression of a visit by an immortal. One could wonder whether the thousand-year visits of the god which is mentioned in Hebrew and other mythologies is in fact connected with time-dilation space voyages, and if the interval between visits was a thousand years, it is possible that an estimate could be made as to the actual distance travelled; and that the solar-type stars within a given radius from our system could then be identified as possible home-stars of the astronauts.

References in mythology frequently mention the seven stars of the Pleiades. This is actually a cluster of some hundreds of stars, but there are seven of naked-eye visibility. These are sometimes said to be the home of the gods, and we have in Hebrew the seven-branched candlestick which has 'heavenly' connotations. Six of these stars in the cluster are bright, and the seventh is fainter, but nevertheless visible. The Pleiades are situated 432-light-years distant, and it is perhaps significant that a round-trip voyage at slightly under relativistic velocities brings us close to a figure of a *thousand years*.

There is another curious legend from ancient India which may possibly have a bearing on the methods employed in conveying colonists from one system to another. Traditions handed down to the Brahmins — the priestly class of India — say that Lunar Pitris created life on this planet after their descent to Earth from the Moon. This would seem to suggest that the first men originated on the Moon, and the Brahmin tradition does name the Moon as the cradle of life on Earth, and claim that it is much older than the Earth. This seems odd, when it is considered that the Sun is usually thought of as the principal life-giving deity. It is also interesting to note the statement that the Moon is older than the Earth, in the light of investigations made by the first Lunar expeditions of the Apollo series, which have led some scientists to the conclusion that the Moon's surface composition is so different from the Earth's it may have originated outside the Solar System, and that it may also be much older than the Earth. When the first Apollo astronauts left the Moon they jettisoned the 'Lunar Bug' after they had docked with the return capsule, and crashed it on the surface of the Moon. The impact caused unexpectedly severe and long-lasting reverberations which immediately suggested that the Moon was hollow, in fact a hollow sphere, and as yet no alternative explanation of the extraordinary echoes has been found acceptable. Yet the idea that the Moon may be hollow is itself so extraordinary that this hypothesis also has been found unacceptable to many scientists, as there seems no way in which a body, according to celestial mechanics, could have been formed hollow. It must therefore have been accomplished by artificial means, and the idea that the Moon could have been altered by the action of intelligent beings is not one that can be accepted at present by our scientists.

Suggestions have been made that long-duration space flights could be undertaken without the necessity to build huge spaceships, whose construction on the surface of the Earth would give rise to insuperable problems of lift-off from Earth's gravitational pull, and which would therefore have to be assembled in orbit round the Earth or the Moon. The alternative is to modify some of the larger asteroids which orbit between Mars and Jupiter, and use these as vehicles. These, it is thought, could be hollowed out, fitted with life-support systems and propulsion units, and used as spacecraft. The advantages are considerable: the rocky shell could be of a thickness to give adequate protection against cosmic radiation and micrometeorites; and a roughly spherical shape would be the ideal for long voyages in free-fall conditions. Spinning the asteroid as it travelled would also provide an artificial gravity, which, although less than Earth-normal, would create relatively comfortable conditions for the travellers, for an extremely long voyage in gravity-free conditions would mean great difficulty in re-adjusting to a planetary gravitational field. The difficulties in carrying out the work of hollowing out such an asteriod and fitting it with its support-systems and propulsion units would be no greater than those of building a huge ship in Earth-orbit from the vast amount of materials which would have to be ferried from the surface. Admittedly, the distance to the asteroid belt is much greater than from a point in Earth-orbit, but by the time we are ready to initiate projects to ferry people to other solar systems the distance factor will have been greatly reduced by faster and more efficient propulsion systems.

This idea gives rise to a thought which is startling, but neither impossible nor impractical: did some other race in the past consider a similar solution and modify a large uninhabited body and propel it through space from another planetary system, a body which later became our Moon? There are some peculiarities about the Earth–Moon relationship, which have no counterpart in the rest of the Solar System. No other planet except Earth has such a large satellite, and it has properly been described as a twin planetary system rather than a planet and satellite system. Where the other planets of the system are concerned the planet is invariably hundreds of times the size of any of its satellites, whereas the Moon is only a fifth the mass of the Earth. Also there are indications that at some time in the past the Earth did not possess a Moon, and it is thought that the Moon is actually a 'captured' body, caught at some time in Earth's gravitational field. Was the capture not accidental however, but deliberate, the vehicle parked in orbit at the end of its voyage, as we ourselves do with our artificial satellites?

A vehicle the size of the Moon would be able to transport a large number of colonists, together with plants and animals which could all be transported to the surface of the new world.

It may sound fantastic, but it does seem rather odd that

some aspects of the Indian legend connect with modern discoveries about the Moon; and the hypothesis could also relate to other origin myths, about the long darkness, and about the egg, or the sphere, as connected with human origins.

Scientists were once of the opinion that voyages to the Moon would solve many problems which could not be solved by observational methods from Earth alone. The results of the surveys conducted have however created more problems than they have solved, and the mysteries of the Moon are perhaps greater now than before the astronauts went there. Whether some of the mysteries of the Moon will be solved by future astronauts only the future will show, as many strange things have been reported by observers over the years. Many have claimed to have seen odd things on the Moon through telescopes, and reports by trained and serious observers cannot be taken lightly. Moving lights have been observed, and domes which appear and disappear. There was a cross formation photographed by Robert E. Curtis, an astronomer of Alamogordo, published in the *Harvard University Review*, and a strange block photographed by Sond 3 in July 1965 and given prominence in *Pravda*. Then there is the matter of what are known as the Blair Cuspids. The attention of William Blair, a specialist in physical anthropology at the Boeing Institute of Biotechnology, was drawn to some photographs taken by Lunar Orbiter 2 of the western edge of the Sea of Tranquillity and published by NASA on 2 November 1966. They are a group of monoliths on the lunar surface which cast very clear shadows, the tallest being some 213 metres in height, and the others about the height of large spruce trees. These formations have attracted the attention of scientists on previous occasions, but have been dismissed as purely natural formations. People have thought they have seen buildings, bridges and even canals on the Moon, which have proved to be perfectly natural features distorted by tricks of light and shade – and perhaps some imagination! But about the Cuspids, Blair said:

If the Cuspids really were the result of some geophysical event, it would be natural to expect to see them distributed at random: as a result the triangulation would be scalene or irregular, whereas those concerning the lunar objects lead to a basilary system, with co-ordinates x,y,x, to the right angle, six isosceles triangles and two axes consisting of three points each.

Blair was asked if he considered this formation to have been the work of intelligent beings. 'Do you want me to confirm it so that you can discredit me?' he replied. 'Well, I will tell you this: if a similar thing had been found on Earth archaeology's first concern would have been to inspect the place and carry out trial excavations to assess the extent of the discovery.'

Of course, this formation could be a natural formation of such regularity as to *appear* artificial. 'But if this axiom had been applied to similar structures on Earth,' said Blair, 'more than half the Maya and Aztec architecture known today would have still been buried under hills and depressions covered in trees and woods ... "a result of some geophysical event"; archaeology would never have developed and most of the facts relating to human evolution would have remained veiled in mystery.'

Perhaps one day explorers will visit this particular part of the Moon and investigate this mystery, and prove whether the formation is natural or artificial. If natural, another phenomenon will have been solved; if artificial, we shall have to wonder what purpose it served. Was it perhaps a navigational device, or a message? And for whom? Was it connected with the mathematically-aligned megaliths on Earth? If so, this would point to visits to the Moon at a period we call pre-historic. Only time will solve this, and other enigmas of the Moon.

However, whether or not it proves that the Moon was originally a giant space vehicle, space vehicles travelling to Earth *could* have been of completely artificial origin, and it is a fact that the design of long-duration space vehicles now under serious consideration will be thought of in spherical or egg-shaped terms, as these shapes are considered optimum for interstellar travel. In this way, of course we are copying nature; most interstellar natural bodies are globular in shape. Freud has said that the sphere or the egg is one of the oldest archetype images in the human subconscious; and this may in fact stem from an ancestral memory of such vehicles. The golden egg which descended from the sky is a theme of some mythologies, particularly from the Pacific and Easter Island.

We also have to consider a common human experience in dreams of the floating or flying sensation, which astronauts have likened to their experience of weightlessness in space. This sensation is so exhilarating that astronauts have frequently to be warned about their reluctance to terminate their 'space walks'. Certain areas of experience, stemming from the deep unconscious and revealed only in the dream state, are reckoned to be ancestral memories, inaccessible in the conscious state. There is a degree of uncertainty regarding the floating sensation, so akin to the idea of levitation, and one explanation offered suggests that it stems from the time when all life lived in the sea, where the effect of the Earth's gravitational pull is not as noticeable. However, this subconscious phenomenon does seem to have more in common with the astronauts' experience, and may in fact relate more to an ancestral memory of the time when human beings travelled in space in a state of weightlessness.

Descriptions of the vacuum of space; dreams of weightlessness; golden eggs from the gods in the sky – it is curious to note here that our space vehicles are coated with gold foil, a reflective agent to prevent absorption of excessive heat. Do not these things point to a possibility that in the past Earthbound man was Cosmic Man ...

3

Fall of Angels

The Flood is a world-wide legend; the condition of the world and of humanity *before* the flood is also the subject of much world-wide mythology, and legends from many different points of the globe have many points of convergence. It is generally recognised that the Flood legends of the New World were not diffused from the Sumerian/Babylonian myths, and therefore it seems possible that a planet-wide catastrophe occurred which is dissociated from the localised floods of the Tigris–Euphrates delta. We can therefore postulate that the state of the world before the Flood, independently described by many different groups from all over the world, must have had a basis in reality.

Common is the theme of a vanished Golden Age, which perished with the Flood. Also widespread is the idea that before the Flood Man had access to a great deal of knowledge which made the Gods fearful, so that they caused the destruction of the majority of the human race and the knowledge was lost. There are accordingly two main themes behind the reason for the apparently Divine visitation of the Flood – Man's wickedness, which is stressed in the Biblical Old Testament; and his acquisition of great knowledge, which is emphasised only as 'sin' in the Bible. We can seek elsewhere in mythology for the knowledge referred to, and find an Indian tribe in South America who say in their legends that men learned how to fly and so the Gods destroyed them. In the Maya Popol Vuh it is said that the 'First Men' could see what was far and what was very small, and they surveyed the four quarters of the globe. The Gods closed the eyes of the first men, and all their knowledge was lost.

It is logical to assume that if an advanced civilisation was largely destroyed during a planet-wide catastrophe, most of their knowledge would be lost as the survivors reverted to savagery.

We can infer the existence of such an advanced civilisation, which was probably World-wide in extent, partly from legend and partly from certain evidence, both material and documentary. First, we shall deal with the legendary evidence.

The myth of Paradise before the Flood is common to all the ancient Middle Eastern cultures, the most familiar of course being the Biblical Garden of Eden where there was no sickness or knowledge of sin. The Sumerian legend is almost identical to the Biblical description; the Sumerian poem quoted is called by Dr Kramer the 'Epic of Emmerkar':

The Land Dilmun is a pure place, the Land Dilmun is
    a clean place.
The Land Dilmun is a clean place, the Land Dilmun is
    bright place.
In Dilmun the raven uttered no cry.
The kite uttered not the cry of the kite.
The lion killed not.
The wolf snatched not the lamb.
Unknown was the kid killing dog.
Unknown was the grain devouring boar.
The sick eyed says not 'I am sick eyed.'
The sick headed says not 'I am sick headed.'
Its (Dilmun's) old woman says not 'I am an old woman.'
Its old man says not 'I am an old man.'

In the Semitic version of this myth, Dilmun was the dwelling place of the immortals.

We note this close similarity between the Sumerian and Hebrew myths: the absence of sickness, and the lack of predators so that the domesticated animals were always safe. It may not be as important to argue whether the Hebrew was a copy of the Sumerian myth, or whether they developed independently. What is important is that all these myths speak of a *condition* which existed. If this had been mere wish-fulfilment, surely the ancient chroniclers would have said:

'One day there will be no sickness, and the lion will not kill the lamb, etc. ...' They all appear to be quite convinced that this state of affairs existed at a period before the Flood. Why, then, should we automatically assume that this was merely a story?

We can, I think, make a parallel between our own and Biblical times. If we could transport a dweller from the Palestinian desert region from about 1000 BC to present-day England, what would his impressions be, and more important, what impressions would he take with him when he was returned to his own time?

He would find a countryside so thoroughly cultivated it had the appearance of a garden. He would find the cattle and sheep perfectly safe in their fields, so safe that they could be left unattended all day. No wolves, lions, bears or eagles here. The people would seem so free of diseases as to be miraculously healthy: no trachoma or leprosy, plague or cholera, those common scourges of primitive times.

Would he not, in fact, be describing the legendary Paradise we have described to us by ancient authors?

Of course, *we know* our world is no paradise, but it may seem so, in retrospect, to our descendants, if they should revert to savagery and the world to wild and uncultivated nature. An advanced civilisation in the remote past may have enjoyed conditions similar to those prevailing today.

By the same standards, the people of this civilisation would be as free from disease as we are today. We are not, of course, disease-free; we have our problems with cancers, heart ailments, etc. But the killer diseases of the past have been virtually eliminated from the civilised countries. There is no leprosy or cholera, tuberculosis has been virtually eliminated, bubonic plague and typhus are rare events and swiftly dealt with.

The basic problem we have to face is: how did such an advanced culture come into being at such a remote period?

If humanity had colonised this planet from another world in space, then they would have brought with them, if not the apparatus of that civilisation, at least its *knowledge*. Perhaps these remote ancestors of ours from the stars came here

already completely disease-free and with greatly extended
life-spans.

There is a consistent theme running through all legendary
sources regarding the people from before the Flood. This is
that they were descended from the Gods, and in many instances, were a hybrid of Man and God.

Quoted here is an excerpt from *Middle Eastern Mythology* by S. H. Hooke[1]:

> The myth of the union between divine and mortal
> beings, resulting in the birth of demi-gods or heroes, is
> found in the early Sumerian and Babylonian sources
> whose influence on Canaanite mythology appears in the
> Ugaritic texts.
>
> Behind the brief and probably intentionally obscure
> reference in 6 : 1–4 there lies a more widely known myth
> of a race of semi-divine beings who rebelled against the
> gods and were cast down into the underworld. The
> beings called Nephilim in verse 4 (Genesis) and ren-
> dered giants in the Septuagint and Authorised Version,
> seem to have been regarded by the Yahwist as the off-
> spring of the union between the 'Sons of God' and the
> daughters of men mentioned in verse 1. The assembly of
> lesser gods, so often referred to in Sumerian, Babylon-
> ian and Ugaritic myths, have been transformed in
> Hebrew myth and poetry into the 'Sons of God' con-
> ceived of as a kind of heavenly council over which
> Yahweh presided. Compare for instance, the scene in
> the first Chapter of Job, where the Sons of God come to
> present themselves before Jahweh (Job 1 : 6). Traces of
> the myth are to be found in Numbers 13 : 33 where the
> Nephilim are represented as the survivors of a race of
> giants whom the Hebrews found in Canaan when they
> came to settle there. Another possible reference occurs
> in Ezekiel 32 : 27, where a slight emendation gives us an
> allusion to the Nephilim. In apocalyptic literature and
> in the New Testament (2 Peter 2 : 4; Jude 6) the myth
> has been still further transformed into the myth of the
> fall of the angels, so splendidly portrayed by Milton.

1. Penguin, 1963, page 132.

The fragment of the myth here preserved by the Yahwist was originally an aetiological myth explaining the belief in the existence of a vanished race of giants, but the Yahwist has made use of it here to support his account of the progressive deterioration of the human race, and goes on to connect it with Yahweh's purpose to destroy Man from the face of the Earth.

There are three principal threads running through this mythological series. One is the existence of a race of semi-divine beings. The second is the casting down from heaven of this race of beings (sometimes regarded as giants) and the instance of them being 'chained in the Earth'. And the third is the progressive deterioration of the human race.

How did ancient peoples happen to devise such a complex mythology? A mythology of a race of supermen destroyed in a Flood, of the destruction of most of the human race and the gradual degeneration of the survivors? Surely these myths must be based on factual events, no matter how distorted.

If we were to assume that mankind had originated from space borne colonists, as suggested by some of the myths of origin, then these colonists could have become, in the course of time, associated with the Gods who came from the sky. These earlier generation 'Space Gods' would, once settled on Earth, produce children. Would this perhaps be the union between the 'gods' and terrestrial Man? Later generations would be regarded as the product of gods and men, and thus semi-divine.

An interstellar space-travelling society may, by its very nature, be composed of beings of (to us) greatly extended lifespans. As a civilisation develops its sciences, one of its aims would be the conquest of disease and the ageing processes. Hand in hand with the advancement of the medical sciences would go the progression of the technological sciences. Long-distance space travel may well go hand in hand with such progress in medical matters. Long-duration space voyages would more easily be accomplished by creatures with greatly extended lifespans. A space voyage which we may undertake lasting thirty years is half the life time of a present-day terrestrial human; to a being with an average lifespan of five hundred years, such a voyage would be relatively short, and of little consequence where the ageing of the astronaut is concerned.

It is possible that by the time we are ready to undertake long-duration interstellar flights in manned vehicles, the problem of ageing may have been largely solved, and human life-times dramatically extended.

It is perhaps pertinent to point out at this stage that the Old Testament tells us that the generations before the Flood possessed greatly extended lifespans, and although the ages mentioned in Genesis of some individuals cannot be taken perhaps too literally (Adam was reckoned to have lived for 930 years, Seth 912 years), they do point to a belief that the generations before the Flood lived greatly extended lives. Such a belief may well have been based on fact – we cannot deny that a superior civilisation may have conquered the ageing process; if such a thing were impossible we would not be attempting at this time to discover the cause of ageing and arrest it.

The belief in the existence of giants, or a race of giants, is widespread in many mythologies, including those of the Middle East and of the Aztecs and Mayas of the New World. One explanation for this belief may stem from the many odd ruins which the people who devised the myth will have seen: ruins built on a cyclopean scale and constructed of blocks weighing scores and even hundreds of tons. The people of 2000 or 3000 BC were quite incapable of raising such structures and may well have thought they had been built by giants. One may consider the Pyramids of Egypt, great artificial mountains, constructed of blocks weighing up to ten tons and with beams weighing more than fifty tons; the cyclopean temples of Malta, with blocks weighing hundreds of tons; and the terrace of Baalbek in Syria, also constructed of massive blocks. The vast scale of the pyramid complex at Teotehuacan in Mexico inspired awe in the Toltecs, the forerunners of the Aztecs, and huge-scale construction is common in the ruins of the Inca Empire. Similarly, in Europe legends exist of giants, and here too there are great structures made of massive stones, such as Stonehenge, the chambered tombs and the dolmens. Right up to late Medieval times it was commonly thought that these had been built by magic (and therefore, according to the early Church, by demons) as ordinary people lacked the ability to raise such structures. People lacking any kind of technology could well think such structures to have been erected by giants, as only they would have the strength to move the stones. It is perhaps significant that many of the legends regarding giants stem from areas where such ruins exist, and in many cases are associated with them.

Whether such giants actually existed in fact is doubtful, although some gigantic skeletons are supposed to have been discovered: the discoverer invariably says that the bones crumbled to dust once exposed to the light of day, which seems odd, as other bones, including those of long-since extinct dinosaurs, have survived exposure to the air. It is possible that a race of people existed in the past taller than the majority of present-day peoples, as skeletons of what are regarded as early true Homo Sapiens, called Cro-Magnon, are on average some six inches taller than we are, and have a larger cranial capacity. But it is doubtful whether such people could be regarded as true giants, and it is much more likely that it is the handiwork of an earlier race that gave rise to the legends, rather than a memory of giant peoples.

Can we formulate a hypothesis to explain the rebellion of the semi-divine beings (sometimes called Nephilim) who were cast into the Underworld? If we start from the premiss that there existed in the remote past a highly advanced civilisation, possibly extra-terrestrial in origin, we can postulate that the legend is actually a gross distortion of real events.

We have just to consider the basic tenet we have advanced: namely that the semi-divine beings were actually the descendants of a space-travelling civilisation, and therefore that there existed elsewhere the civilisation that had sent them here. If this planet had been selected for colonisation by a Superior Community, then those distant beings would be aware of the existence of a culture developing here. Further, we have to consider the possibility that when this civilisation became established, it in turn developed (or re-developed) space travel; and that contacts and communication existed between them and the Superior Community elsewhere in the Galaxy. Was the destruction of the human race in the Flood, and the casting down of the semi-divine beings, the result of a conflict between these two civilisations? This may possibly explain the legends of the War in Heaven, the War of the Gods, which is related to the episode we have just mentioned.

We may mention in this connection that certain passages in the Old Testament can be brought together and related to such an episode.

There are several curious statements in the Old Testament, particularly in Isaiah, which have never been properly understood. Consider, for example, this:

13:4 and 5: 'Hark, a tumult on the mountains of a great multitude.

'Hark, an uproar of kingdoms, of nations gathering together.

'The Lord of Hosts is mustering a host for battle. They come from a distant land, from the end of the heavens, the Lord and the weapons of his indignation, to destroy the whole earth.'

Also, Isaiah 13:13: 'Therefore I will shake the heavens, and the earth shall move out of her place, in the wrath of the Lord of Hosts, and in the day of his fierce anger.'

These two passages would seem not to be related to any localised events, but connect more closely with the Flood destruction in the Genesis narrative. Isaiah also says that the Earth shall be laid waste, and men become more rare than fine gold.

The description of a Lord who came with un-named fearful weapons and a host from a *country at the end of heaven* has never been properly understood or given a satisfactory explanation; but translated into modern terminology, does it not sound like an arrival from another world in space? A country at the other end of heaven – thus may have ancient peoples unfamiliar with astronomical truths have described another world in space. The passage which says that the Earth shall be moved out of her place has often been considered to be a fanciful description of an earthquake, but this may not be so, as earthquakes are mentioned freely in the Old Testament, and in more readily understood terms. There is a great deal of evidence to show that a great catastrophe in the past (as opposed to the Ice Age Theory) could have been caused by a disturbance to the Earth's orbit around the Sun.

Much of the Old Testament is a record of catastrophes, and this applies also to Revelations which concludes the Bible as a whole. These catastrophes fall into three groups, or three main events, which are: the Flood episode in Genesis, the Plagues of Exodus, which are connected with the great volcanic eruption on Thera (Santorini) in 1500 BC, and a great destruction *which is to come*.

Most of the world's mythology devotes a great deal of space to *two great disasters*, the Flood episode, and a great disaster at some time in the future. Vedic, Tibetan, Maya, Inca and Aztec mythologies were much concerned with the future destruction, and the Earth's history was divided into World Ages, or cycles of disasters.

How did they arrive at such conclusions, and why did they all consider there was a great disaster to come, which would utterly change the face of the Earth?

It is possible to formulate a hypothesis regarding these legends, but only if we assume the occurrence of a planet-wide catastrophe in the past connected with a cosmic event, either natural or artificially engineered.

The past destruction of a highly advanced civilisation in the past by a global disaster would still leave survivors – it obviously has, or we should not be here today. Some of these survivors, the scientists and mathematicians, would wish to estimate the extent of the disaster which had overtaken the planet, and to this end they devised the mathematical and astronomical complex of which Stonehenge is part (perhaps either the central part, or that part which has survived today in a most complete form). Their calculations would show that the Earth had been disturbed in its orbit, and that this disturbance, by moving the planet into an *outward* spiralling path, would lead to a disastrous situation for survival of life on this planet in thousands of years to come. The world would most likely become very slowly colder, until the time came when survival would become difficult. This minute movement of the Earth, operating now for 6,000 or 8,000 years, has led to a slow and steady deterioration in the world's climate, and it is possible that this could worsen during the next several thousand years.

This is not mere fantasy or idle speculation, as it is obvious that the climate is deteriorating; many areas of the world which once harboured prosperous cities are now deserts, and many of the deserts are growing larger. The planetary temperature as a whole is steadily lowering, for tests have revealed that the ocean temperatures are lower than they used to be. The Antarctic Ice Cap is enlarging at the rate of many millions of tons of ice a year, and far from emerging from a hypothetical Ice Age at the termination of the Pleistocene, we seem to be moving steadily into colder conditions. It has been thought recently by meteorologists that one possible cause could be that the Earth is *moving slightly away from the Sun*, although they do not suggest a prior cause as to why this should be happening.

I say it is this factor, this ancient *mathematical and astronomical knowledge*, distorted now into a religious symbolism, which is the truth behind the Armageddon concept. The knowledge which was transmitted that the Earth had been started on a course to disaster has, over the ages, been transformed into a religious-orientated prophecy of divine vengeance and punishment.

We have already observed that the Old Testament and Revelations are concerned with three disasters, where mythologies from other parts of the world mention *two*, and this seems to point to the one (Exodus) being a localised phenomenon, and the other two planetary events.

Not only Genesis, but many of the prophets, are much concerned with the destruction of mankind by these catastrophes, and this applies also to Revelations. It would appear from this Biblical summation, if one may use the term, that this is a compound of the Flood legend, the Thera eruption, and Armageddon (the disaster to come).

We note in Revelations 12:7: 'Now war arose in heaven, Michael and his angels fighting against the dragon and his angels, and the dragon and his angels fought, but they were defeated and there was no longer any place for them in heaven. And the great dragon was thrown down, that ancient serpent, who is called the Devil and Satan, the deceiver of the whole world – he was thrown down to the earth, and his angels were thrown down with him.'

Revelations 20: '...And he seized the dragon, that ancient serpent, who is the Devil and Satan, and bound him for a thousand years, and threw him into the pit, and shut it and sealed it over him, that he should deceive the nations no more, until the thousand years were ended.'

It is necessary here to relate this to the statements contained in Genesis. We remember in our quote from *Middle Eastern Mythology* that the Nephilim were a race of semi-divine beings who were God's servants who dwelt with him in heaven, then *rebelled and were cast down*. Therefore, the Nephilim and Satan and his (fallen) angels *are one and the same thing*. As the casting down of the Nephilim took place during the *Flood disaster*, then this passage in Revelation refers obviously to Flood events.

Therefore, the War in Heaven between God and his angels, and Satan and his angels, is part of the Flood episode, and shows – supported by mythologies from elsewhere in the world – that the Flood itself was an effect of a vast planetary disaster.

We have postulated that this catastrophe was not natural, but more probably artificial, involving weapons of appallingly destructive powers. There exist descriptions of weapons which appear to resemble nuclear bombs. Even an ancient description of radiation sickness is clinically accurate (see the Mahabharata).

This possibility of a nuclear holocaust in the distant past raises some interesting points if we are attempting to interpret part of the Revelations statements, particularly those dealing with the fallen angels and Satan being cast down and sealed under the ground for a long period of time. Biblical numbers appear to have been ritualised – the forty days of rain of the Flood, Christ's forty days in the Wilderness, the 1,000-year visits of the God, and the casting down of Satan and his angels for 1,000 years. One suspects that the one stands for a short period of time and the other a long period of time, and that they are not to be taken too literally.

We postulate that the War in Heaven was an actual war, possibly using nuclear weapons. In a nuclear conflict, one of the protections from radiation would be to build shelters deep underground – this is the sort of precaution we ourselves have envisaged against a nuclear disaster. In such a war in the remote past, it is logical that such shelters would have been built, not to protect the mass of the people, but to shield the scientists and the leading members of the government against the day when it would be safe to emerge and commence the task of rebuilding civilisation. The passage in Revelations 20 could in fact be not a mythological event, but real – the casting down was, in fact, hibernation in deep shelters against radioactive contamination. As we are all aware, radiation effects can be lingering, and radioactive cobalt, for example, has such an extremely long half-life that a cobalt bomb could render its point of impact uninhabitable for 50,000 years because of lingering lethal radiation. It may have been necessary for those 'entombed' in these shelters to stay there for many years, perhaps even several generations, until the radioactivity level had dropped to tolerable limits. Can we not suggest therefore, that the sealing of Satan and his angels in a pit for a thousand years was in fact the subterranean incarceration of important representatives of that civilisation?

There is in fact startling verification of such an idea. What would be more likely to support such a hypothesis than the discovery of deep underground shelters? We have already suggested that the so-called passage graves were in fact hastily constructed shelters either against attack or against the devastation resulting from the catastrophe. But it has now been shown that deep artificially constructed shelters do in fact exist. Erich von Daniken, in his book, *Gold of the Gods*,[1] has revealed the existence of a network of tunnels and caverns, at least partially artificial, or artificially enlarged, almost a thousand feet below the surface in Ecuador, South America. The fact that these deep underground chambers were built and occupied by man has been proved by the

1. Souvenir Press, 1971.

artifacts found within. In a huge chamber the size of a modern aircraft hangar were a large table and chairs made of an as-yet unknown material. Golden statuettes, and some three thousand leaf-thin gold metal plates inscribed in an unknown language, were also found. The inscriptions on the plates, which seem to be more alphabetical than heiroglyphic, would appear to bear a resemblance to ancient Cretan Linear script and Sanskrit; and this fact in itself seems to point to an extremely ancient written alphabetical language, completely unknown to us, which has undergone great transformations in the course of time, becoming in the course of time the alphabetical languages of the ancient world.

Underground chambers and tunnels, built on a megalithic scale, have been found in Turkey (the site of Man's most ancient identifiable settlements), and underground passages exist beneath the cyclopean structures at Sacsayhuaman above Cuzco, in Peru.

Daniken's explanation for these extraordinary underground chambers is that they were built by spacemen who visited this world thousands of years ago, as presumably any people indigenous to this planet were incapable of such feats. Why should it be assumed that everything extraordinary should be constructed by visitors from another world? It has even been suggested that the pyramids and Stonehenge were built by aliens from elsewhere because these structures do not fit with the picture we are given of the capabilities of our remote ancestors. Weighing up the mass of other evidence – the Flood legends, the Age of the Gods, and the suspicion that there existed a superior civilisation in the distant past – does it not seem more likely that these places were built by terrestrial humans in an attempt to ensure the survival of at least some of the human race against the dangers of a vast disaster? What possible reason could spacemen have had for building such places? Surely if danger threatened them, all they had to do was to take off.

It is these places which could have been the *pit of Revelations*. Possibly, many more such places await discovery in many parts of the world.

The tunnels in Ecuador were first discovered by an Argentinian scholar, Juan Moricz, following clues supplied by Ecuadorian Indian folklore. Similar legends exist among the Indians in the Maya region of Central America, which tell of underground cities and tunnels stretching for miles beneath the ruins of the ancient Maya centres. Perhaps in the light of this new evidence, we should not be too hasty in discounting these legends.

Does the discovery not also throw a new light on the widespread legends of the Underworld, where dwelt the Gods of Darkness? We have suggested that the gods of the sky were either Earth-men travelling in aircraft or in space, or astronauts from elsewhere in the Universe. The Underworld gods, by the same reasoning, were those members of a superior civilisation who had been forced to live underground for great periods of time, while their less fortunate contemporaries had to endure the hostile conditions of the surface, bereft of civilisation, reverting to barbarism, and distorting truth into legends.

The Sumerians had their legends of the Underworld, where they described the journey of Inanna, Queen of Heaven, to her sister Ereshkigal, goddess of the Underworld.

The Babylonian form of this legend is that of Tammuz and Ishtar.

In Ugaritic mythology Baal visits the Underworld.

The Egyptians had their legends of the Underworld, as also the Maya, the Celts and the Nordics. In fact, there is scarcely a place on Earth where this myth does not exist in some form or other.

It is thus possible that these legends were based on facts, although as in many other examples of myths based on fact, they were distorted and incorporated within the general framework of religious myth and ritual.

We are brought to a further point, and that is to the emergence of those mysterious figures, the Culture Gods, or Culture Bearers. In every story the building up of an ancient civilisation has been accomplished with the help of these godlike figures, who guided their savage followers to the paths of culture. They were the ones who taught building and metalwork, agriculture and irrigation, mathematics, astronomy and law.

Osiris of the Egyptians was a lawgiver and the teacher of healing.

Wirakocha of the Peruvians taught the arts of civilisation, plant and animal husbandry, building and irrigation.

Kukulkan of the Maya and Quetzelcoatl of the Toltec/ Aztec taught all the arts of civilisation.

Each of the Greek gods had his special skill which he taught to Mankind.

The Babylonians had their legend of the Apkullu, who taught their ancestors the rudiments of civilisation.

Whence came these strange superior beings?

Some, it is said, came from the sky. Others apparently came from nowhere. If they had emerged from their long incarceration in *secret chambers deep underground, it could well have been thought that they had emerged from nowhere.*

The Gods from the sky, and from the darkness deep underground: perhaps they both played a part in leading their barbarous descendants once more to the light.

4

World in Decline

The myth of the degeneration of Man, characterised in Genesis by the decline following the Flood, is also a world-wide phenomenon, although in varying forms. The wording may be different, the general impression given is the same. Such myths are common, as may be expected, throughout the Middle Eastern and Mediterranean civilisations, where possibly one has influenced the growth of the other, but they also exist in one form or another in many parts of the world.

In the sacred book of the Maya, the Popol Vuh, it is said:

> They looked into the distance and could discern everything which was in the world. When they looked they saw everything around and the dome of the sky and the inside of the Earth. Without moving themselves they saw everything hidden in the distance. They saw at once the entire world, from the place in which they stood. Their wisdom was great. Their eye reached every forest and mountain and lake, every hill, sea and valley. Verily, they were wondrous men.
> The Gods said: Let us satisfy their desires a little, for what we see is not well. Must they resemble us in the end, their creators who know and see all from the distance?
> So the gods cast a veil over their eyes so that they grew dim as when the breath touches a mirror; they could see only that which was near at hand and clear. Thus was destroyed all the wisdom and knowledge of the first men.

These First Men, also called the Saiyam Uinicob (Old White Fathers) were reputed to have built the first cities that were destroyed in the Flood.

South American Indian tribes have the legend of the time white men had learned how to fly, and the gods became afraid that they would rival them and destroyed them, nearly all.

Constantly there is this theme of Man's former greatness, his almost-destruction, and the reduction of the survivors to ignorance, deprivation and disease.

The thing that concerns us now is: can we establish a basis for belief in the ancient myths that a superior humanity has degenerated and may even still be degenerating?

There is a certain amount of evidence which could point to a degeneration of the human species, and we could draw conclusions from some factors in the present human condition to support such a hypothesis.

We are all aware of the great ages attributed to men in the period before the Flood and mentioned in Genesis. Such legends also exist in Sumerian and Egyptian mythologies. We are also aware that there is, in Genesis, mention of a systematic reduction in the lifespans of the generations following the Flood. We have already mentioned (in *Colony: Earth*) that this would be a logical sequence if humanity were on the road to degeneration. Each generation would be less healthy than the one which preceded it, and a decline in lifespan would be a natural consequence. The present lifespan is some seventy years – and this in spite of all our advances in hygiene and medical techniques – which is exactly that mentioned in the Bible for the 'present' generations of Man. In the less well-developed societies such as those in India and Africa, the average lifespan among the native populations is *half* of this. Actually, what we in the West have achieved is not a prolongation of life but, by better living standards and medical care, insurance that a majority of our citizens survive the hazards of existence to reach this Biblical age. Actual extension of the lifespan has not been achieved.

We have already mentioned the advantages of an extended lifespan for a space-travelling community, and suggested that colonists to Earth from such a community could have possessed these extended lifespans, which fact could have given rise to the legends about the demigods from the Golden Age.

It may well be that there are areas of evidence for supposing that Man may once have been a longer-lived species than at the present time.

First, let us consider that remarkable mechanism, the human brain.

It has been estimated that there are some ten thousand million grey cells, or neurons, in the brain. Each neuron contains upwards of 20 million RNA molecules (RNA molecules are the DNA 'messenger' molecules) and each RNA molecule is capable of handling millions of 'bits' of information. It has been estimated that during a normal human lifetime the human brain absorbs some one million billion (1^{15}) 'bits' of information. As Isaac Asimov, the famous American science writer and biochemist, has said:

There is no question, then, that RNA presents a filing system perfectly capable of handling any load of learning and memory which the human being is likely to put upon it – and a billion times more than that quantity too (*New York Times Magazine*, 9 October 1966).

It would seem, therefore, that the average human being of today utilises only the minutest fraction of the brain's potential, and that there are large areas of the brain which lie dormant, and have no known function. Yet possibly everything we experience and learn in a lifetime, down to the most minute and insignificant detail, is stored away permanently somewhere within this small, yet vast, organic memory storage unit. It is known that under hypnosis, or sometimes in dreams, information can be brought to the surface from the subconscious which cannot be reached by the conscious mind, or by a conscious act of will in the normal way.

Occasionally we hear of people who possess remarkable memories, or who can handle enormous numbers and compute huge and complex sums in their heads almost instantaneously, which would take most people weeks to work out on paper if they could do it at all. There is the example of Miss Shakuntal Devi of India, known as the Human Calculator, who was asked by the University of New South Wales in Australia to appear in a contest against UTECOM, one of Australia's biggest computers. In Sydney in 1959, Miss Devi was asked: 'Find the cube root of 697,628,098,909.' The Indian girl gave the answer in seven seconds – 8,869. The computer provided a slightly different result, which was wrong, and only as a re-run provided the correct answer. The experts were amazed.

There have been other examples of people who can juggle with figures in this extraordinary way – they seem to behave like computers.

One could say that an electronic computer is a large-scale version, or imitation, of the human brain, containing only a tiny fraction of the relays contained within the brain. A computer containing several million relays is capable of producing calculations, in a matter of seconds, which would take teams of mathematicians months to compute using paper and pencil. Yet these computers can handle only a millionth of the information the human brain can absorb. The difference lies in the fact that the memory section of the computer can, on instruction, instantly be recalled, whereas in the case of the human being the greater part of the memory circuits are locked away in the subconscious and are inaccessible.

If the human brain functioned as efficiently as an electronic computer, then a human being should be able to recall every detail of everything he has ever learned, and, furthermore, should be able to analyse and compute from this data. As we have seen, there are a few people, who by a 'freak' of nature are able to do this on a limited scale. But are they really the freaks, or is it the rest of us who are the freaks? When one considers the way the brain functions, or rather should function, and compares it with an electronic computer, which is an electronic version of the brain, then, if our potential were realised, we should all be able to act in this way. The way the few gifted brains function is not at all understood, but the answer seems to lie in the way the recall system operates, which in 'normal' people appears to function at a low level of efficiency.

If full use of the potential of the brain was realised, then books and all written records would be no longer necessary – information would at all times be available to us. No subject would need to be learned painfully and slowly over the years, as a thing once learned would never be forgotten. Recorded information would only still be useful, perhaps, as a way of preserving for posterity.

Yet it must be taken into account that, even if the potential of the brain were realised, it would still be capable of absorbing vastly more information than could be gathered in the present normal lifespan of some seventy years. Possibly a man could live for a thousand years and still not reach the full potential of the brain's information intake.

It would appear on balance, then, that the brain was designed for a creature with a vastly longer lifespan.

If we concede that the human brain is not utilised to its full extent, does this point to an evolving organ? According to the evolutionary theory, animals evolve from simple forms to those more complex, and this should hold true of human beings. These changes are reckoned to take place over periods of millions of years, and yet Homo Sapiens appears to have 'evolved' explosively over a period of less than half a million years. The 'explosion of mind' as it is termed by the anthropologists, was accomplished so rapidly (by geological reckoning), as to be almost instantaneous. By this same reckoning, the human brain should be developing, and there should be noticed, over the last six or seven thousand years, an appreciable increase in individual human intelligence. But there is no evidence to support such a view – rather the reverse.

The brain size of Modern Man varies from 1,100 cc and averages out between 1,350 cc and 1,500 cc. What have been termed our first true ancestors, Cro-Magnon, who lived some 30,000–35,000 years ago, had a larger-sized brain than Modern Man. The so-called 'Old Man' of Cro-Magnon had a brain capacity of some 1,600 cc. *Time* Magazine of 19 March 1961 gave the brain capacity of Neanderthal Man as 1,625 cc, considerably greater than present-day humans.

On average, both Cro-Magnon and Neanderthal Man had a brain as large as, or larger than, Modern Man.

Cro-Magnon was first discovered by the French archaeologist Louis Lartet in a rock shelter in a cliff face near the village of Les Eyzies in the Dordogne in 1868. The shelter was called Cro-Magnon, hence the name assigned to the skeletons of the people discovered there. Analysis of the skeletons showed them to belong to people with long straight limbs, of an average height of more than six feet. The forehead was exceptionally high and domed, and the brow ridges were so reduced as to be almost indiscernible.

We now turn our attention to Neanderthal Man, whose origin is no less obscure than that of Modern Man, and about whose pedigree there is considerable discord in anthropological circles.

Homo Neanderthalensis is so named in honour of a seventeenth-century German theologian called Joachim Neander. In honour of his abilities as a writer of hymns, the citizens of Dusseldorf named a valley near the city the Neanderthal, and in this valley the first bones of Neanderthal Man were discovered. The discovery was made by workmen cleaning out a limestone cave, and most of the skeleton was thrown away by them as worthless, the surviving parts being a skull cap, some limb bones, a few ribs and part of a pelvis. A Dr Fuhlrott of Eberfeld collected these specimens and Prof D. Schaaffhausen of Bonn gave the first scientific description of them.

This Neanderthal, known as the conservative type, has been pictured as follows: erect walking, stocky and barrel chested, with his head sunk somewhat between exceedingly broad shoulders, short legs, powerful arms and the head with a receding brow and chin which seems too large for the body.

However, many kinds of Neanderthal Man have been found, and they appear to have occupied as wide an area as Cro-Magnon, or modern-type Man, being found all through Europe and the Middle East. The Ehringsdorf and Steinheim skulls from Germany, and those from Mount Carmel and other places in Israel, appear to be more modern in appearance. The Ehringsdorf skull possessed the heavy brow ridges, but was high-domed as are the Cro-Magnon skulls.

Briefly, the anthropologists divide Neanderthal into two classes, the 'Conservative' rather like the traditional picture of an apeman, and the 'Progressive' which seems to be a combination of 'ape-type' and Cro-Magnon. It has also been found that Neanderthal and Cro-Magnon (or Homo Sapiens) existed at the same time, and it has been thought that there may have been a degree of interbreeding between the two types, with, in the end, Homo Sapiens, represented by Cro-Magnon, absorbing or eliminating Neanderthal. If it is true that these two types could interbreed, it must mean also that they were from a common stock, and not divergent lines of development, because fruitful unions would not otherwise have arisen. But it is a little difficult to imagine that the advanced-looking Cro-Magnon, who had, apparently a more 'intellectual' appearance than even we ourselves, would mate with the Neanderthal of 'Conservative' type as he has been pictured by the anthropologists – a shambling hairy brute differing little in appearance from the apemen reconstructions we have been shown – particularly as there would have been Cro-Magnon females for the males and vice-versa.

The age of Neanderthal Man is still a very open question, but in view of the possibility of both conflict and hybridisation with Cro-Magnon, he falls within the chronological period of true humanity. It is generally assumed that he will have lived between 160,000 years ago and 35,000–40,000 years ago, being supplanted thereafter by Homo Sapiens.

Neanderthal Man, in spite of the apelike portrayals given us by the anthropologists, nevertheless had some extremely human characteristics. He was familiar with fire and used stone tools, although it has been the opinion of some experts that some of the stone flakes which have been taken to be tools are actually natural objects. If he was familiar with fire, it can be assumed that in addition to using it to keep warm and to keep wild animals at bay, he may have cooked at least some of his food. There have been found round balls of stone in association with Neanderthal, and it has been thought that these may have been heated and placed in water as a cooking aid.

It is also thought that he lived in rough shelters or tents made of skins, and that he also used skins as clothing to protect himself against the elements.

There is little evidence to show that Neanderthal possessed any form of art, or whether he had any spiritual beliefs of any kind, but in some European caves of Mousterian times skulls of cave bears have been found associated with Neanderthal remains, and arranged in a way which suggests a ritual of some kind. For instance, in the Petershohle, in the South German Alps, a number of cave-bear skulls were set in niches in the cave walls. Some experts are of the opinion that there may have been a cave-bear cult equivalent to the bear cults existing among primitive tribes in the far north of Europe today.

It is also certain that Neanderthal had a great respect for their own dead, as skeletons have been found laid in graves shaped to fit the body, sometimes with a ring of animal bones surrounding it, and in one case the skeleton still shows traces of having been covered with flowers. A curious feature of many Neanderthal burials is that most of them show the corpses orientated with the heads pointing to the west. This has been taken by some anthropologists to show that they were buried with a degree of ritual which can only be described as religious, and may show that Neanderthal had some idea of a heaven, comparable to the Egyptian concept of the land of the dead at the setting sun – in the west.

We can see that there are many peculiarities regarding Neanderthal Man – the conflicting number of types, which seems to vary between the 'ape' type and true humans, the fact that he used clothing and tools, possibly built shelters, and apparently had some form of religious belief and ritual. Is the picture presented to us by the anthropologists of a primitive 'half man' a true one, we may ask? Is there another explanation for Neanderthal Man?

Originally it was suggested that Neanderthal Man was stooped, and walked on bent legs – rather like a modern anthropoid. The view was modified when it was put forward that the distortion of the limbs could have been caused by illness such as arthritis due to the cold and damp conditions under which he lived. Now, it is thought, Neanderthal Man in health was as upright as a modern man. Were, we may think, *all* the deformities caused by disease of some kind, and is what we are looking at, in fact, a *distortion* of a true human being caused by disease? We remember the large brain capacity of Neanderthal, larger than that of a present-day human, in a creature whose bulk was virtually the same as that of a present-day man: less in some instances, as the average Neanderthal skeleton averages 5 ft. 5 in. Even if this average height is deceptive because of bone malformation, the brain/body ratio is far greater than that of any animal except man.

The skeletons of what we term Neanderthal are thus those of true human beings, severely affected by disease, whose distortions have been taken as evidence of a separate, primitive offshoot of the human type. The enormous variation in skull type, from exceedingly primitive in appearance to those almost of Cro-Magnon, could have been malformations brought about by bone disease or genetic malformations by mutation. Remember, the totality of remains we have discovered numbers barely sixty persons in all, and many of these remains are testified to only by a few bones, or in some cases by a part of a skull only. Before we 'invent' a new race, or new races on the strength of such small evidence, we ought to question the existing hypotheses and suggest a new one.

We mentioned malformation by mutation, and this leads us to another idea, which has a connection with some peculiarities of Palaeolithic Man, and also with our next chapter.

Mutation. Generally, today, we associate mutation with two specific causes – malformation of the genetic structure by chemicals (as in the case of Thalidomide), or by irradiation by natural or artificially induced radiation.

We have suggested that there may have been a nuclear conflict in the past, and several writers have brought this concept to our attention in recent years. Daniken mentioned the use of nuclear weapons in his book *Chariots Of The Gods*, and the theme was explored also in Tomas' book *We Are Not The First* and by Kolosimo in *Not Of This World*. Even as far back as 1909, Prof Soddy mentioned the possibility that nuclear science may have been attained by a race so remote in time that it has left no record in history.[1]

We stated two reasons for radiation damage in the past; and one was the use of nuclear and possibly other weapons,

1. *The Discovery of Radium*, Murray, 1909.

which, either separately or in combination, brought about a movement in the Earth's former orbit around the Sun. If the Earth had orbited in a more circular path, or slightly nearer to the Sun, this would have meant a warmer planet, with the possibility of a higher rate of evaporation, thus creating a high-altitude 'blanket' of water vapour. This vapour layer would have had the effect of filtering out excessive radiation: it is possible that the level of natural 'background radiation' is higher now than it used to be in the past.

It has been suggested that one of the causes of ageing is this continual bombardment by background cosmic radiation experienced by all organisms. It is known that all radiation has a harmful effect on living organisms, and it is thought that this irradiation, although not deadly to life, is in some way responsible for the slowing down of cell replication processes, which is one of the reasons for ageing. Of course, there are other factors in the ageing process, such as the accumulation of toxic substances in the organism which also contribute to the slowing down of cell replication, and natural wear and tear will also play a part. However, radiation possibly plays a major part in the ageing process, by slowing cellular replication in the first place, and therefore making it more possible for other factors to cause damage than would otherwise have been the case.

A nuclear conflict in the past would have created a sudden upsurge of radiation levels, which would eventually have exhausted itself, thereafter leaving a higher level of natural background radiation. When could this event have taken place?

We cannot say for sure, but we can make a guess to within several thousand years, taking into account certain factors.

It has been discovered that the cores taken from the bed of the Ross Sea in Antarctica indicate that the glaciation of Antarctica commenced some 6,000 years ago. Examination of vegetation of subtropical type found in these cores indicates that the plants died about this time, due to the climatic change which had taken place.

Similarly, fossilised orange and magnolia trees have been

discovered in the Arctic regions, some thousands of years old.

The commencement of civilisation on this planet has been dated around 4000 BC in many parts of the world. This includes the Egyptian, Sumerian, the Indus Valley civilisations and possibly also some of the pre-Inca cultures of South America. Some Mayan remains in Central America have also been assigned dates almost as old as those of Sumer. All these civilisations have a tradition of a great catastrophe, observed in Western cultures as the Flood.

It is likely, therefore, that the Catastrophe, which some have equated with the termination of the last Ice Age, occurred between 6,000 and 8,000 years ago (6000–4000 BC).

According to this hypothesis, then, both Cro-Magnon and Neanderthal remains are not nearly as old as had been thought, but are more recent by many thousands of years. This is not to say that Man has not existed here for many thousands of years, and the figure of 35,000–40,000 years for the existence of Homo Sapiens may be almost accurate. On the other hand, Man may have been here for tens, or even hundreds of thousands of years longer than this, *in a highly civilised state*, traces of which scarcely exist today.

Some mythologies record that the Age of the Gods lasted for hundreds of thousands of years (Egyptian and Sumerian), pointing to a tradition in antiquity of an enormously extended period of civilisation in the remote past.

Neanderthal and Cro-Magnon remains have been found in association with the bones of the great cave-bear, the mammoth, woolly rhinoceros and the Mastodons and other antique elephants of Asia and America. As it has been thought that these animals died out tens of thousands of years ago, it must therefore be assumed that the remains of 'primitive' man are of similar antiquity. But is this really so? If all these species of animals, which are thought to be so ancient, were destroyed in a vast catastrophe, and this catastrophe occurred some 6,000 or 8,000 years ago, then our dates have been placed much too far back in time. A congress of scientists in the Soviet Union dined off mammoth steaks, as some of these creatures have been found frozen in the ice in a perfect state of preservation. Surely they could not have been there for 40,000 or 100,000 years? Also representations of elephants have been found carved on stelae in the Mayan region of Central America, and it is thought in some circles that the American elephant may have vanished only during the past 10,000 years, with an occasional specimen surviving even into historic times (the last 2,000 years).

It may be true that all the skeletons we have found of what we term primitive Man, both Cro-Magnon and Neanderthal, living harsh lives in caves and by hunting, were the degenerate survivors of this great disaster, and that most of them date from between 8,000–6,000 year ago.

We suggest, then, that what we have taken for a primitive form of Man (Neanderthal) living both prior to Homo Sapiens and within the period of Man, was in fact the distorted mutation of True Man himself. The Neanderthals were descendants of normal human beings, living in highly irradiated areas following the holocaust and subject to severe mutation effects caused by radiation. In time, of course, the most severely affected would die of radiation sickness and there was probably also a high degree of sterility. But, as the radiation was dissipated, humanity slowly reverted to the norm, with the aberrant specimens dying out. *This would explain the disappearance of Neanderthal Man.*

There is evidence of a use of nuclear weapons in the Americas as well as in Asia, and should it not therefore be supposed that we should find traces of Neanderthal-type Man in the Americas, if the causes of their condition were radiation sickness? We have not found any such traces, and indeed there have not been any traces of any apelike humans in the Americas. It may be that they are still to be discovered, or perhaps the survivors left the more badly contaminated regions before they could become so affected. There is a degree of evidence to show that traces of Homo Sapiens in the Americas are as ancient as those in the Old World, so it is something of a mystery as to why there are no Neanderthal type remains. This is as yet an unresolved mystery.

We say that Mankind reverted to the norm. But it was a norm which exists today, and *not* the norm which existed prior to the disaster. The norm *then* had an extended life-span and a vastly superior intelligence.

Ancient Man (whereby we include both Cro-Magnon and Neanderthal) generally had a larger brain than possessed by Man today, as we have seen. Of course, brain size in itself is no direct guide to intelligence, as the more important guide to intelligence is the degree of convolution, or folding, of the cortex. However, from the shape and position of the skull features, it is thought that Cro-Magnon Man's brain was as highly developed as Modern Man's, only larger. This could point to a degree of natural intelligence higher than that of the present time.

Some scientists have thought that since Cro-Magnon, the human brain has been decreasing in size. Dr Ernst Mayr has said that the trend may now be in a downward direction – development of the brain stopped 100,000 years ago. This seems to point to a degeneration of the human species, and not, as is inferred by evolutionary theory, to an advancement.

We are faced with this curious phenomenon – if the human brain is in a developing state, why are there areas of the brain which have no known function, and why are our brains not used to a greater extent? If we were developing, sections which are non-functional *would not yet exist*, but the brain would instead gradually enlarge over the generations as human intelligence increased. We have seen that the reverse is the case. Therefore, does it not seem more likely that the brain has to a certain extent atrophied, or lost much of its function over the centuries?

There is another mysterious peculiarity to be found in extant remains of ancient Man, and that is evidence of trephining, an operation in which a section of skull is removed to examine the brain, to relieve pressure, to remove a damaged part caused by a tumour, or to remove bone splinters caused by skull injury. Such operations today are extremely delicate and dangerous, and require the highest surgical skills. In fairly recent times, when the operation was carried out at the Hôtel Dieu in Paris in 1786, it was invariably fatal.

Yet the Man we term Palaeolithic carried out a great

number of such operations, judging from the skulls found which had been so treated, and from the healing that had taken place it must be assumed that the individuals not only survived the operation but lived for many years afterwards. When one considers that the number of human beings from the remote past whose remains we have discovered is remarkably small (all the members of Homo Sapiens found so far would not populate a small village), the number of trephinings carried out was proportionately extremely large. It has also been dicovered that in South America, a great many successful trephining operations were carried out by pre-Inca surgeons at least 2,500 years ago. Why did ancient Man carry out such a great number of trephining operations? We are given the usual explanations – it was done to let out devils, or as part of some ritualistic magical ceremony, or even for the cannibalistic purpose of eating the brains of an enemy. The last explanation seems exceedingly doubtful in view of the number who survived the operation. Of course, it is admitted that some of these operations may have been carried out for medical reasons, since brain damage may have been a frequent result of Stone Age Man's habit of knocking his enemy over the head with a club! But this is a mind-boggling picture: people who would indulge in such barbarous violence at the same time having surgeons capable of carrying out such delicate and skilled operations? They must have had a more serious reason.

It is being increasingly realised that Stone Age Man was nowhere near as primitive as he has been painted, and we will go so far as to say that there was in fact no such thing as Stone Age Man. Because people may have been thrust into a primitive environment by certain events, and have had to improvise with the most basic of tools, is no reason to assume that they must therefore have *been* primitive. The megalithic structures which abound throughout Europe and which stem from a time far removed from those stages of civilisation we term the Bronze and Iron Ages represent a high order of intelligence and mathematical ability. In fact, since we are baffled as to how some of these structures were erected, they could point to a mastery of certain techniques of which we are ignorant today.

In a so-called burial barrow in Southern England a set of metal implements were discovered recently which could not be readily identified, and were eventually found to be a set of surgical instruments closely resembling those in use by surgeons at the present day. Do these instruments stem from the period when the barrow was built, or were they left there by later people who used the structure? In some of these barrows have been found the remains of fires, cooking utensils and other household implements, and it looks as if their use was originally other than as burial grounds. They may have been shelters for the *living*, and if some of those living were injured it would explain the presence of the medical instruments. It also means that our divisions of Stone, Bronze and Iron Ages are very loose descriptions and should not be taken too literally. After all, we have today a civilisation that makes space rockets, and in other parts of the world, Stone Age cultures – such as that of the Aborigines of Australia. In 1,000 years time, if the evidence for our civilisation had vanished, and all the archaeologists discovered were the stone tools of the Aborigines, they may well come to the conclusion – and it is hardly necessary to say a false one – that the twentieth century was a Stone Age period. Surgical instruments in the period *we* call the Stone Age may seem incredible, but surely far less incredible than the vision we have been offered of a trephining operation carried out on a human being by bits of flint hammered away into a human skull, without the benefit also of any anaesthetic – and the patient surviving afterwards!

If it were true that the brain capacity of man has decreased, and perhaps also his intelligence, then the people who carried out all these trephining operations – these people who were the survivors of the collapse of a highly advanced civilisation – would want to know why intelligence was decreasing. They may have wondered why their memories were failing, why they were unable to carry out mathematical calculations with their former precision, or why they were subject to severe head pains and tumours. Were they, in fact, carrying out these numerous operations partly to try to discover what was going wrong, and perhaps also try to discover the cause of so many cancerous tumours?

Radiation sickness has been frequently described – loss of hair, lassitude, vomiting, weakness and eventual death. It is also known that the first of the cellular structures to be affected are the brain cells. If there was a high level of radio-activity due to nuclear fallout, it is possible that there could have been a high incidence of brain damage, coupled with a loss of faculties.

Further, the increased radiation, both from fallout and the higher background radiation, could have been key factors in lowering the lifespan of the human race, as we observe in Genesis that after the Flood there was a systematic decrease in the lifespan of the generations.

The possibility of a high radiation level at a particular time in the past brings us to another point. It was suggested by L. A. G. Strong in his book *Flight To The Stars* that perhaps the various monsters encountered by the ancient Greek heroes, such as Jason and Ulysses – we remember the Cyclops with one eye in the middle of his forehead – were actually mutations caused by radiation from a star ship's engines. Strong hinted that there was a possibility that the gods and monsters of Greek myth may actually have been spacefarers visiting this planet (anticipating Daniken!) and that mutations may have occurred as a result of a too-close proximity to the ship's atomic-powered engines.

Perhaps there is a more terrestrial answer, and that such mutations were a result of a nuclear holocaust on this planet. We are reminded that our mythology and traditions are peopled with many odd monsters – ogres and hairy sub-men, people with horns on their heads, satyrs with the feet of goats, were-people, vampires. Many of these legends are difficult to trace to their source, and seem to stem from a particular point in history, in the same way that all the world's major religions seem to have come into being at a certain time. Could it be that all these varied monsters, both human and animal, were in fact the victims of massive exposure to radiation? Of course, such creatures no longer exist, and so the traditions are dismissed as fairy tales. But, like the birth of the gods, *something* must have triggered off such ideas – there seems no reason, *at the source*, why such tales should have been invented. Perhaps then, such creatures did in fact exist, but do so no longer because they eventually died out, as do all mutations unfitted for survival, and the race reverted slowly to normal, leaving behind a memory of distorted creatures to linger in the uneasy sub-conscious of the human race.

5

A Nuclear War – 5000 BC?

A nuclear war some 6,000–8,000 years in the past? A fantastic idea – an impossibility? This idea, which would explain many mysteries about our past, and which at one time would have been dismissed out of hand, is being considered as a serious possibility today. I have myself heard it said by laymen – people whose minds are uncluttered by dogmatic scientific ideas – that an atomic war in the past would explain many things which are at present not understood. Perhaps the layman has hit on truths which are obscured by the trained scientific mind's over-rationality.

Before the dawn of our own atomic age, many puzzling features of the earth, and some aspects of mythology, could not have been explained by such an idea, simply because we were unfamiliar with atomic weapons and their capabilities, so the idea would not have occurred to us. Until we had started to experiment with radioactive substances, could any living person on this planet have described radiation sickness? No, for the simple reason that such a disease did *not exist*, and therefore could neither be described nor diagnosed.

Yet – radiation sickness, in clinical detail, is described in an ancient Sanskrit text, the Mahabharata. Such an affliction could not have been described unless it had been experienced, otherwise how would the ancient chroniclers have been able to describe it so precisely?

The Mahabharata describes with crystal clarity the explosion of great fireballs, the gales and storms which they created, and the after-effects. These take the form of hair loss, vomiting, weakness and eventual death: classic symptoms of radiation poisoning. Even more significant, it is said that persons in the vicinity of these weapons could save themselves by removing all metal from their persons and immersing themselves in the water of rivers. There could be only one reason for this – to wash away contaminated particles, the same procedure followed today.

There seems to be a high degree of proof, in various forms, that nuclear science was known in the past.

First, there is the context of the Mahabharata, frequently cited by modern writers. Daniken mentions the description of nuclear weapons from this ancient text, and his explanation is that they were used by advanced aliens from space against the primitive people of this world. It seems somewhat unlikely that an advanced race would go to such measures against primitive people who had weapons no more elaborate or dangerous than spears and bows and arrows.

The Siddhanta-Ciromani, a Brahmin book, subdivides time until it reaches a final unit, truti, which is 0·33750 of a second. Sanskrit scholars are puzzled why such a small unit of time was used in antiquity, or how it could have been measured without instrumentation. Modern-day primitive peoples are notoriously vague about time, and even hours have little meaning for them. There is no reason to suppose that primitive peoples from the past should have viewed time any differently, which makes it even more puzzling.

Tomas, in his book *We Are Not The First*[1] says, in his chapter 'From Temples and Forums to Atomic Reactors':

According to Pundit Kaniah Yogi of Ambattur, Madras, whom I met in India in 1966, the original time measurement of the Brahmins was sexagesimal, and he quoted the Brihath Sakatha and other Sanskrit sources. In ancient times the day was divided into sixty kala, each equal to twenty-four minutes, subdivided into sixty vikala, each equivalent to twenty-four seconds. Then followed a further sixty-fold subdivision of time into para, tatpara, vitatpara, ima and finally kashta – or 1/300 millionth of a second. The Hindus have never been in a hurry and one wonders what use the Brahmins made of these fractions of a microsecond. While in India the author was told that the learned Brahmins

1. Souvenir Press, 1971.

were obliged to preserve this tradition from hoary antiquity, but they themselves did not understand it.

The time unit of kashta – 1/300 millionth of a second – is absolutely meaningless without instrumentation and, more significantly, is close to the lifespans of certain hyperons and mesons – *atomic particles*.

The Varahamira Table, dated approximately AD 550, gives a mathematical figure which compares closely with the structure of the hydrogen atom. Were these figures also handed down from a more distant time?

The Yoga Vasishta says: 'There are vast worlds within the hollows of each atom, multifarious as the specks in a sunbeam.' This seems to hint at the knowledge not only that matter is made of numberless atoms, but that the atoms themselves are, as we now know, mostly *empty space*.

These writings, which stem from a remote period, hint that knowledge of atomic physics existed in the past. The fact that the Brahmins were *obliged* to remember these mathematical symbols, even though they did not understand them, represents an effort to transmit knowledge from a vanished technological era. One can imagine scientists observing their civilisation collapsing, writing down their knowledge, and entrusting a certain group always carefully to record and pass the information down the centuries, until the time should come when it would be understood once more. Much has been lost; what has survived has survived only in fragmentary form. But although hidden in monasteries, or in obscure texts which have never been brought to the attention of scholars, there may still exist much more information about nuclear physics. As it has happened, we have discovered the nuclear age for ourselves by a separate route, although perhaps it may have been better if the knowledge had never been rediscovered.

Something of this ancient knowledge seems to have filtered down through the ages in a more generalised form, because Democritus the Greek, 2,500 years ago, proclaimed: 'In reality there is nothing but atoms and empty space.' However, the Greek thought that the atom was the smallest unit of matter and could not be divided, whereas

Moschus, the Phoenician, who had acquainted the Greek with this information, asserted that the atom could be divided.

Lucretius of the first century BC, a Roman scholar, wrote that atoms 'rushed everlastingly through space, and underwent myriad changes under the disturbing impact of collisions. They were too small to be seen.'

After the collapse of the Roman Empire, it was not until the nineteenth and twentieth centuries that serious work on atomic physics was undertaken.

Of course, these ancient scholars, whose fragmentary knowledge must have stemmed from a remote and forgotten technical age, could not demonstrate their theses in practice. The technology did not exist whereby they could do so.

That remote age where nuclear science was practised must have used atomic energy for many purposes; and some of the ideas of more recent times, such as transmutation, which the alchemists kept alive in their endless search to turn lead into gold, may have originated in the ancient knowledge that manipulation of atomic structures could convert one element into another. The fact that the alchemists strove to do this by a chemical method demonstrates merely that the methods used were in error, not that the concept was invalid.

However, what we are concerned with in this chapter is not the use, but the misuse of nuclear energy. It seems clear that a frightful holocaust occurred in a past age, and writings from different sources confirm this. Whether the conflict was purely terrestrial or involved another advanced race from elsewhere in the Universe is a matter for speculation.

From India we have the evidence of the Mahabharata and the Drona Parva. These speak of the great fireballs; also of Kapilla's Glance, which could burn fifty thousand men to ashes in seconds, and sounds either like nuclear energy used as a beam, or some kind of laser weapon. The Drona Parva speaks of flying spears which could ruin whole 'cities full of forts'.

Flying spears which could ruin cities – could these be missiles, possibly with nuclear warheads?

India is not alone in legends such as these. They exist also in China. Raymond W. Drake says that the legends in the Feng-shen-yen-i describe events which have a close similarity to the Sanskrit Mahabharata. Rival elements fought for control of China, helped by celestial visitants who used weapons whose descriptions remind us of our own advanced technology. The war was fought with blinding rays and dragons of fire, spheres of flame, shining darts and lightning. According to the descriptions, they seem to have possessed something akin to radar, whereby they could see and hear objects many hundreds of miles away. Also used were flying dragons of silver, and chariots of fire and wind. These all seem to refer to laser beams, nuclear weapons, missiles and flying machines using rocket or jet engines.

In Siberian shamanistic legend there is a warrior with dazzling arrows who blows up anyone who laughs at him and rides away through the sky on a 'shell of gold'.

The ethnographer Baker was told by a Canadian Indian, who was a wise man of one of their secret totemic societies, that once there were great forests and meadows 'down there' and also great shining cities and men who flew in the skies to meet the thunder-bird. Then the demons came and the cities were all destroyed and only ruins exist now. These legends stem from the regions of perma-frost in the Far North of the Canadian tundra, and they must refer to an ancient epoch when the climate in the polar regions was very different from what it is today. By 'down there' we must assume it was to the south where the shining cities lay.

This Canadian Indian tradition should remind us of the tradition existing among the Maya and Aztecs about the cities where the lights never went out by day and night.

The Maya say: 'These lands (referring to the southern part of what is now the USA) are the Kingdom of Death. Only the souls which will never be reincarnated go there ... but it was inhabited a long time ago by ancient human races.'

There is a great similarity among legends from many different parts of the world – nearer home we have Zeus of the Greeks with his lightning bolts, and the Nordic Thor with his hammer and lightning. If there had been a world conflict in the remote past, wider even in scope than World War II and much more devastating, then surely this is what we should expect. Global conflict would leave echoes in global memories.

In the same way, the legends of the Golden Age are equally widely dispersed. Those who seek a marvellous 'Atlantis' in any one place are, it seems, doomed to disappointment. If the whole world was highly civilised at a certain period in the remote past, then the legends of its former existence will be world-wide in extent. The fact that different legends from all points of the compass have led people to believe that Atlantis existed in the Mediterranean, the Atlantic, Spain, Greenland or Iceland, America or Tibet, or even that a similar kingdom, that of Lemuria, existed in the Pacific, merely means that all these legends, so widely scattered, point to a civilisation that was world-wide: civilisation that was not limited to one mysterious island or continent now sunk beneath the sea. A global civilisation at a *remote* period would explain the similarities between widely separated cultures of antiquity – *and also the differences.* There are broad points of similarity between the civilisations of Egypt and Sumer, the Indus Valley, and those of Central and South America, particularly in their legends, where we know of them. There are also great differences, although these may largely be in the matter of *detail*, such as the Old World possessing the wheel and the New World not making use of it. It should be remembered that at the period of megalithic building, *all over the world*, the wheel was not in use anywhere. Those who would completely debunk the idea of there being any connection *at any point in time* among all the civilisations of the past, both in the Old World and the New, do not seem to be taking all the factors into consideration. However, we seek in vain for one isolated area for our 'mother culture' from which all civilisations descended. The whole earth was the 'mother culture'.

We have a further peculiarity to remark in the old disaster myths. Many of the legends, which point to a great and disastrous conflict in the remote past, point also to the regions where these conflicts took place. *And most of these regions are now deserts.*

The Chinese have their legends: there, in that great land,

lies the unknown Gobi Desert, which hides mysteries beneath its sands. India has its deserts, and where the Indus Valley civilisations flourished is now desert, Much of the South-western United States is desert, where the Maya point to as the Kingdom of the Dead. In Egypt, Horus cursed the Lands of Set for thousands of years, and vast tracks of North Africa, including the great Sahara, are deserts. Much of the Middle East is desert, with the great cities of the Babylonians and Sumerians lying now as ruins under the shifting sands. Australia is mainly desert, and the Aborigines would seem to be descendants of a once highly civilised people. Perhaps here, also, lie buried the traces of cities from long ago.

Legends, mythologies. Texts describing ancient weapons which sound like nuclear missiles, other texts which seem to refer to the mathematics of nuclear physics. The evidence seems to be piling up in favour of our hypothesis. Do we, however, need more than old texts and legends – more concrete evidence to support the intangible? This concrete evidence, also, exists.

When nuclear weapons were test-exploded in the New Mexico desert, and also by the Chinese in the Gobi near Lop Nor, the sand was vitrified (fused into glasslike areas) by the heat of the explosions. Intense heat is needed for this – volcanic action will not produce the same effect, nor ordinary explosives or fires. The heat of millions of degrees, that of thermo-nuclear reactions, is necessary.

The Gobi Desert has areas of vitreous sand which have been there for thousands of years. Similar ancient glassy sands exist in parts of the Californian desert, and the mysterious glassy tektites found in the sands of the Middle East and North Africa are thought to have their origin in radioactive processes. Was it thermo-nuclear heat which produced these ancient areas of glassy sand? Rocks in Peru and Bolivia show evidence of vitrification, and desert conditions exist there also.

Should we not ask ourselves: why do these great deserts exist – what brought them into being in the first place? Why should there be deserts surrounded by huge areas of vegetation on all sides?

Could it not be that these deserts were created in the *first instance* by the exploding of nuclear missiles of great power in these areas, destroying not only those who may have lived there, but all life; and by radioactive contamination sterilising the areas for centuries to come? Little grows in these deserts and all that grows and lives there has special adaptations to the harsh conditions, and survives only with difficulty. Perhaps there is truth in the legend of Horus, and the curse against the Lands of Set was the curse of radio-active poisoning.

It could be said that our hypothesis is faulty if there were no trace that humanity had lived in these now barren regions, that they had from time immemorial been lands hostile to large-scale human settlement. But this is not so.

There are ruins in the Gobi Desert, almost formless and of great antiquity. These ruins bear the marks of blistering by great heat, of the same kind which was noted at Hiroshima.

There are the ruins of a city in Death Valley in California, and others scattered across Southern California to the Colorado River.

'The whole region between the rivers Gila and St John,' wrote a friend of the adventurer William Walker, 'is covered with ruins. The remains of cities are to be found there which must be most extensive and they are burnt out and vitrified in part, full of fused stones and craters caused by fires which were hot enough to liquefy any rock or metal. There are paving stones and houses torn with monstrous cracks which seem to have been attacked at times by a giant's fire-plough.'

'Throughout California and nearby regions' (Oregon, Arizona, etc.) writes Serge Hutin, 'there are odd ruins. Off the coast of Santa Barbara there are islands with the remains of fortification erected by a vanished race, that of the Chumash, which had a brilliant scientific and technological level ...'

Some geologists maintain that many of the present desert areas of the southern United States and their curious rock formations were not brought about by natural causes.

During excavations near Chillicote, Illinois, bronze coins

were dug up from a depth of $42\frac{1}{2}$ metres. This is a considerable depth, and the pressure and the vast period of time which has elapsed since these coins were buried has flattened them and erased all traces of any markings they may once have held.

In 1851 in Illinois, two copper rings were found, at a depth of $36\frac{1}{2}$ metres. In June of that year, a vessel was blown out of pudding stone at Dorchester, Mass. It was a bell-shaped jar made of an unknown metal with a floral design in silver.

A doctor in California found, inside a piece of gold-bearing quartz, a small object resembling a bucket handle. A similar handle was found in a cave in Kingoodie, northern England, in a block of stone, and has been estimated as being 8,500 years old, if not older. One can assume that the Californian find is of similar antiquity.

In 1969, inside a rock from the 'Abbey Gallery' in Treasure City, Nevada, were found the traces of a screw 5·08 cm long. The screw had long since disintegrated, but the space it had occupied left its trace in the shape of spiral thread markings. This was possibly tens of thousands of years old.

A farmer called Tom Kenny in the Plateau Valley discovered, at a depth of 3 metres, a section of pavement made of smooth symmetrical tiles. Analysis of the mortar proved it to be unlike the local valley materials.

All these finds, from North America, point to something which had not previously been considered: that there exist traces, sometimes buried far underground, of a civilisation many thousands of years old, in *North* America, and which appears to have been violently destroyed in a vast catastrophe involving levels of heat which can only be attributed to thermo-nuclear reactions.

Of civilisations in Central and South America, we have evidence in abundance. Were those who founded the earliest elements of these civilisations survivors of the vast cataclysm to the North? The origin of the Toltec and pre-Toltec peoples who built the vast pyramid complex at Teotehuacan are not known, and the Aztec had a tradition of travelling down from the North — from the 'Country of Painted

Colours' which could have been the Grand Canyon region, with its bands of different-coloured rocks.

The pre-Inca and Inca peoples of South America worked in gold, silver, copper and bronze – no other metals. In the sixteenth century Spanish conquistadores found an 18-cm iron nail inside a rock in a Peruvian mine. The rock was estimated to be tens of thousands of years old. Who had made this nail, obviously before the time of the Incas?

Ancient iron nails have turned up elsewhere. A Mr Hiram D. Witt in 1851 discovered an iron nail with a perfect head inside a piece of auriferous quartz. The discovery was made, according to *The Times* of 24 December 1851, when he dropped the quartz, which broke and revealed the nail. Again, in Kingoodie Quarry, where the golden 'bucket handle' was found, an inch of iron nail, including the head, was found embedded in rock. All these stem from a period before metals were used at all, according to the experts.

China, the Americas – here exist the legends of a vast conflict, and here also the evidence. In India, too, where we have the clearest reports of a past high technology, there are strange things.

The explorer De Camp mentions the existence of charred ruins between the Ganges and the mountains of Rajmahal, which seemed to have been subject to intense heat. Huge masses had been fused together and hollowed 'like lumps of tin struck by a stream of molten steel'. A British official, J. Campbell, observed similar ruins further to the south. Other travellers have described ruined buildings made of unusual materials, 'like thick slabs of crystal', and these also had been subjected to extremes of heat, being holed and split by enormous powers. A radioactive skeleton was found in India with a radioactive level fifty times above normal.[1]

Buried under the shifting sands of the deserts there must be many things formerly unsuspected. Perhaps it would be useful to check in these areas for traces of higher radiation than normal. Perhaps the ancient radiation has long since dissipated, but there still may be lingering traces ...

The jungles of India and Central and South America have scarcely been investigated. Both subcontinents, for instance,

1. A. Gorbovsky, *Riddles of Ancient History*, Moscow, 1968.

have areas which have never been thoroughly explored and there are remote villages which have never seen a white man, in spite of the fact that Europeans have lived and worked in India for several centuries, and have built railways and dams and modern cities. These remote and mysterious regions may hold keys to the past.

Do the pyramids of Egypt hold a clue to the riddle of a nuclear holocaust in ancient times? The Ein Shams University of Cairo, under Dr Luis Alvarez, placed a cosmic ray detector in the base of the Pyramid of Khephren for the purpose of ascertaining if there were any chambers in the pyramid which had not been discovered. Cosmic rays shower on the pyramid uniformly from all directions, and if there were any unknown hollow areas within the pyramid, the cosmic rays would pass more easily through these spaces and leave heavier shadow traces in the detector. In September 1968, tests showed the detector to be in perfect working order.

The hundreds of recordings made during 1967–9 were analysed by the IBM 1130 computer at the University, which showed that they had no common daily features. Dr Amr Gohed, in charge of the installation, remarked: 'This is scientifically impossible. There is a mystery which is beyond explanation ... there is some force that defies the laws of science at work in the pyramid.'

In *Colony: Earth* the author suggested, being guided principally by legends – there is no other guide, as the Ancient Egyptians themselves regarded the Pyramids as a mystery – that the Egyptian Pyramids were not tombs, but shelters constructed in the event of a vast catastrophe: not necessarily shelters for human beings, although some may have sheltered there, but perhaps for the safe-keeping of information and knowledge. If the catastrophe took the form of an intelligently directed disaster, including the use of nuclear weapons, then this hypothesis is given added weight by these cosmic ray tests and their strange results. It may appear that the pyramids, in addition to their other attributes as impregnable shelters, were also *radiation-proof*. It may also appear that, whatever device was used for this purpose, *is still functioning*. Is there, as Tomas suggested, a generator situated somewhere beneath the pyramids?[1]

Such a device may be situated deep underneath the pyramid, far below any excavations which have been attempted so far. What form such a device may take, or how it may be detected is difficult to say, because it is beyond our technology, and we do not know on what principles it operates, how large it is, or how it is powered. Indeed, there are still many unsolved mysteries about the pyramids, and yet there are those who still insist that they were merely tombs of the Pharaohs. This is not to say that the author approves or agrees with the more fanciful stories and theories which have been developed regarding these structures. There are some for instance who say that the height of the Great Pyramid of Cheops, multiplied a million times, represents the distance from the Earth to the Sun. In fact, various measurements and figures have been produced from time to time to show all sorts of things – the length of the year, the lunar month, the weight of the Earth. Some have suggested the pyramids were built by Noah after the Flood, or that they were built by spacemen, or on the instructions of spacemen, or that they were guidance-markers for astronauts from other planets. The idea that all the world's knowledge is concealed somewhere within the pyramids, however, may not be altogether fanciful; though it would probably be truer to say that the knowledge possessed by the ancient world *was* placed in the pyramids, but is no longer there. So much mystique has grown up around the Egyptian pyramids, particularly in the last hundred years, that it is difficult to reach a conclusion which lies between the outrageously far-fetched and the prosaic.

We cannot agree with the more wild theories, but neither can we agree with the idea that the pyramids were built by a group of people without the wheel, with scarcely any tools, and no hoists or other weight-lifting tackle, in a country which, at the time the pyramids were supposed to have been built, was almost uninhabited (the population in total is reckoned to have been some two million), possessed no cities and scarcely any trace of any but small settlements.

The author is of the opinion that the pyramids, particu-

1. See *We Are Not The First* by Andrew Tomas, chapter 22.

larly the vast group on the Giza plateau, are pre-Egyptian, were not built as religious structures or tombs, but were protective devices, possibly for the storage of knowledge, much of which was used by the 'culture bearers' when they emerged or returned to lead the savage descendants of the survivors of the catastrophe back to civilisation. In all the pyramids in Egypt, and there are over sixty known, there has not been traced beyond doubt a single burial. All the burials of the Pharaohs, and especially those most important and powerful rulers such as Rameses II and Thutmosis III, were buried in the famous Valley of the Kings. This is where the treasure of the boy king Tutankhamun was found, we remember. It is surprising how many people think that the mummified remains of the Pharaohs were discovered within the pyramids, simply because it has been stated so categorically by the experts that the pyramids were the burial chambers of the rulers of Egypt.

If the greatest and most illustrious rulers of Egypt were buried in rock tombs in a valley, why is it assumed that less important, obscure and by no means always real kings (the ancient king lists of Manetho do not list a Cheops) were buried in these vast edifices, supposedly raised by so much human toil and sweat? The Egyptologists appear to be guided largely by the records handed down by that great traveller of antiquity, the restless Herodotus. But Herodotus was guided by what the guides and priests of his day told him, when the pyramids were already thousands of years old, and as much a mystery to the Egyptians of the period as they are to us today.

It is surely more likely that the true purpose of the pyramids was far from that which has been generally supposed.

In the preceding pages we have discussed the possibility of, and offered the evidence for, a nuclear war in the past. We have seen that not only nuclear bombs may have been known, but missiles and something akin to radar, together with aircraft. None of these things could have been produced without the resources of a highly advanced technology and therefore an industrialised society. We may also assume that this being the case, the lost Golden Age was probably only a Golden Age in retrospect – to the survivors, who probably remembered the benefits and preferred to forget the disadvantages. In reality, however, this lost technological era may have suffered from all the ills which beset ourselves, and indeed, if their inhabitants were so much more advanced than ourselves, their problems may have been that much greater. The fabled cities of light must also have had their slums, traffic problems and noise and stress problems; they also may have had labour and industrial unrest and possibly difficulties with vast populations, over-crowding and the dangers of breakdown of food supply. Even if these people were truly the godlike figures of mythology, with marvellous intellects and long lifespans, there could still have been psychological flaws in their make-up which could have created the same dangerous situation we in our society find ourselves in today.

Perhaps, on highly advanced colonists from another solar system, the radiation from this Sun took its toll. Possibly they suffered a degree of degeneration over the ages – we have mentioned the fact that radiation affects the brain structure more quickly than other parts of the organism. By the time a purely terrestrial conflict was imminent, they may already have started to degenerate, although even then remaining immeasurably superior to ourselves. This aspect would explain the Genesis statement that man became corrupt and that 'evil was in his heart continually'.

On the other hand, they may have perfected a society far more advanced than ours and more humane – perhaps the fault lay in their relations with other races elsewhere in space, and that the catastrophic conflict which wrecked their world and almost destroyed the human race was brought about by a hostile intelligence from another planet, perhaps an invasion from another solar system.

Perhaps it was a combination of all or some of these factors. It may be that we shall never know the exact circumstances of Man's 'Fall' but will have to rely on our interpretation of the mythologies and the available evidence.

It does seem certain that something is sadly amiss in our planetary system, if planetary systems are formed in the manner described by our astronomers. We shall go into this point in detail in our next chapter.

If a past era with a high technology possessed nuclear weapons, missiles, radar, etc., and if it followed a development parallel to our own pattern, their people will also have possessed other methods of waging war. We have evidence from both mythological and material sources that this may have been the case.

An ancient Sanskrit text, the Samara Sutradhara, mentions the development of *biological* weapons in the remote past. Samhara was one which crippled, and Moha induced paralysis. The Feng-shen-yen-i mentions biological warfare used in Ancient China, and again we have this close similarity between these descriptions and those from ancient India.

This could lead us to an interesting thought: is it not possible that certain diseases may once have been artificial in origin? There are many diseases which seem to be exclusive to the human race, and which do not affect animals. V.D. seems to affect only humans, and although indiscriminate sex is blamed for its spread, many species of animals are far more indiscriminate in their sexual relations. Though cholera and typhus are carried by animals, the animals are carriers only and do not seem to be affected. Could these, and other human afflictions, have been artificial in origin? A hangover from ancient biological warfare, raging unchecked when barbarism descended on the world and medical services collapsed, to await the coming of our twentieth century to find once again the cures? It is an interesting thought, because Firsoff has suggested that the virus, which is now regarded as the intermediate stage between life and non-life, may not be so ancient after all. Many biologists point to the virus and say that here we have the prime example of the first stage of the division between the organic and the inorganic world, because the virus in its inert state behaves like a crystalline formation (the inorganic) and when active it replicates and behaves in a purposeful manner (the organic). Firsoff has mentioned the high degree of 'host specifity' of the virus, which could point to it being a recent development. In other words, some viruses have a high degree of host specifity to the human host, and as human beings are reckoned to be a recent arrival on the planetary stage, the virus can be regarded as similarly recent. We can go a step further and suggest that perhaps certain viruses were originally 'tailored' to attack human beings by being artificially created in the laboratory. Viruses have recently been synthesised in modern research laboratories, and therefore it is not impossible that a highly advanced society in the past did a similar thing. This would connect closely with the reports of biological weapons in ancient documents.

We will now consider another example of ancient weaponry which also exists on our present society, and this is the projectile weapon, such as the pistol, rifle and high explosive.

A human skull was discovered in a cavern in Northern Rhodesia, and is now on display in the Museum of Natural History in London. There is a perfectly round hole in the left side of the skull and the right side is shattered. There are no radial marks – the hole is perfectly round. This effect, a perfectly round hole and the opposite side shattered, is typical of that of a high-velocity rifle bullet. A spear or arrow head would not cause such a hole, neither would it create the shattered effect on the opposite side – only a hot, high velocity projectile can do this. This skull has been estimated as being *40,000 years old*! Yet we are told that Man, at this stage, had only just appeared in the world, and had not even invented the bow and arrow.

This skull is not the only ancient example of a peculiar injury.

The Palaeontological Museum of the USSR possesses a skull of an auroch which is many thousands of years old. An auroch is an extinct type of cattle which was supposed to have vanished from the earthly stage tens of thousands of years ago, yet this ancient animal skull has a perfectly round hole in the front of the forehead, and examination has shown that the creature, although injured, was not fatally so, and the wound had healed. Like the Rhodesian human skull, the hole was perfectly round with no splintering effect, such as would be caused by a rifle bullet.

Rifles in the remote past – could it be possible? We have the concrete evidence, and we are reminded of certain references in mythology: to rods which can spit fire. Moses had a rock which let water forth when he struck it. It *could* have been a divining rod – water divining is an ancient art – but it could have been a projectile device. There are old myths also from Druidic times which talk of rods which spit fire and can kill. We know that Moses was brought up from babyhood as a member of the Egyptian ruling class, and may have had access to knowledge restricted to the rulers and the priestly class. It is something of a mystery how the Ancient Egyptians managed their excavation work in driving tunnels through solid rock, as in the Valley of the Kings and the building of the Abu Simbel 'House of Eternity' which Rameses II had built into a cliff face. It has been suggested that in the earlier periods of Egyptian history there was a knowledge of explosives which was later lost. This is not as strange as it may seem – China was making explosive powder several thousand years ago, although they did not put it to any practical use. The possession of firearms in remoter periods is not as odd as it may seem, therefore, and to a civilisation which possessed nuclear weapons, the use of rifles and other similar weapons should not seem at all remarkable.

An even more remarkable suggestion has been made by some Soviet scientists. Some unearthed skeletons of dinosaurs seem to provide evidence, in the nature of the fractures and the position of certain bones, that they were shattered by the use of high explosives. This of course would place the use of explosives (by someone) many millions of years in the past, and here we are reminded of an earlier suggestion in this book, which is that the dinosaurs may have been deliberately destroyed by Man either before or during colonisation of the planet.

Clearly, the knowledge of and use of explosives and weapons based on explosives is immeasurably more ancient than we have always supposed.

Finally, we shall turn to another mystery which may well have a connection with a nuclear holocaust in the remote prehistoric past; that of the meaning of certain cave paintings and rock drawings scattered around the world.

These so-called spaceman figures have received considerable publicity in recent years. They were first popularised by Daniken in his book *Chariots of the Gods*, and have also been mentioned by many other writers.

The most well-known drawing is the giant outline carving on the Tassili Plateau in the Sahara, discovered by Henri Lhote, and christened by him 'The Great Martian God'. It could, perhaps, hardly have been christened anything else – the resemblance to a figure in a spacesuit is quite remarkable. There are other drawings in the Tassili region which are very similar, one showing a group of four figures walking, who appear to be wearing something like spacesuits, complete with bulbous helmets.

Drawings like these have been found in many parts of the world. There is a rock drawing 40 km south of Fergana in Uzbekistan (USSR) which shows a figure with the head enclosed in a ring with rays coming from it, which could represent a transparent 'fishbowl' helmet with antennae. There are almost identical figures in Val Camonica in Italy. 'Spacemen' figures have also been found drawn on rock faces in Australia.

The 'Dogu' statuettes from the Jomon period of Japan too have aroused considerable interest. These statuettes represent people wearing protective clothing of some sort, together with helmets with curious eyepieces. Isao Washio, the Japanese expert on these figures, says: 'The gloves are fixed to the forearms with a rounded attachment while the eyepieces can be opened or closed. There are levers at their sides perhaps meant for manipulating these, while the "crown" on the helmet is probably an antenna ... the designs on the suits are not ornamental but correspond to devices suitable for regulation of pressure automatically.'

All these drawings and figures are today being associated more and more clearly with spacemen, and the possibility that this planet has been visited by astronauts from other worlds in times past. They may in fact be representations of our early 'sky gods', and the fact that the figures are often associated with flying devices – discs, or spheres in which they are sometimes enclosed – would appear to add weight to the theory. At an ancient astronomical observatory at Meroe in the Sudan there is even a perfectly clear drawing of something which appears to be a tapered rocket or missile, complete with antenna.

While it is agreed that there is a good case for seeing these figures as spacemen, there could however be another explanation. Are they, perhaps, people wearing protective clothing – decontamination suits against radioactive pollution.

We may observe that many of these drawings of 'spacemen' images have been found in what are at present *desert* areas. We have already suggested that perhaps the deserts were created, in the first instance, by the use of nuclear weapons, so they would still have been dangerously radioactive some thousands of years ago. The pictures could have been drawn by surface-dwelling survivors who had regressed to savagery, while the suited figures were visitors on survey missions, who had arrived by some sort of flying machine either from areas not so severely affected by contamination, or from their deep underground shelters. We are aware that there exist many legends of Man's possessing flying machines in the past Golden Age, so the fact that the suited figures are associated with aircraft or other flying devices does not necessarily mean that they are extra-terrestrials.

In fact, not only do legends of flying machines survive from the remote past, but in 1972, near the Step Pyramid in Saqqara, there was discovered under the sand a wooden model of what appears to be an aircraft, very similar in design to a modern jet aircraft. The object was dated as in excess of 5,500 years old, and one daily newspaper dubbed it 'Tutenconcorde'. Although most experts thought it was merely a rough model of a bird, this seems to me unlikely, since the Ancient Egyptians were perfectly able to depict the shape of birds – the most popular one being the emblem of Horus, a hawk – and this object looked exactly like a rough wooden representation of an aircraft, the sort of thing someone not very good with his hands may make for a small child, or the kind of thing a child himself would make.

Of course, some of these drawings may represent visitors from other worlds; but we cannot overlook the possibility that the protective suits were worn by terrestrials as a shield against radioactive contamination. If people from other planets had to be so thoroughly protected against the terrestrial environment that they wore fully insulated spacesuits, it would be most likely to mean that they were unable to breathe our atmosphere, or tolerate our temperatures. But this does not fit in with our picture from mythology of the sky gods, their appearance and behaviour. If it is assumed that the ancient gods were spacemen, they include Wirakocha, Quetzelcoatl and Kukulkan of the Americas, and perhaps also the gods of the Egyptians, Greeks and Hindus. These are never described as wearing protective suits. So they must either have been terrestrials, or aliens from other worlds whose physiology was so similar to that of terrestrials that they did not need spacesuits. Of course, short-stay visitors may have worn spacesuits as a protection against unfamiliar solar radiation hazards or contacting unknown and possibly highly dangerous terrestrial micro-organisms.

However, on balance, considering the location of the principal drawings, and the evidence offered for a past nuclear holocaust, protection against radiation hazards may seem the more reasonable explanation.

6

Clash of Worlds

It is now generally assumed by astronauts that solar systems are probably the rule rather than the exception where solar-type stars in the Universe are concerned; and that there are possibly many millions of planetary systems in our Galaxy alone. The reason for this opinion, as against the earlier assumption that solar systems were extremely rare, is that newer concepts have been developed on how solar systems are formed. At one time, it used to be thought that a wandering star pulled a filament from the Sun as it passed close by, and that this filament later condensed into the planets and moons of our solar system. This line of reasoning meant that as such near-collisions were extremely rare, planetary systems would also be rare. However, the general design of our planetary system does not equate with such a theory. A newer explanation proposes that solar systems are formed by the condensation of a cloud of gas and dust – the 'cold accretion theory'. A cloud of dust and gas would thus condense into globules and rotate around a centre of gravity by centrifugal force, the central part or core forming the Sun, and the condensation of the outer parts forming the planets and moons. This proto-system, with its whirlpool, *almost* admirably fits the present shape of the Solar System, and although it is not altogether satisfactory, it is the most reasonable of all the alternatives offered to date.

Basing their reasoning upon our solar system, astronomers have devised a model for a 'life-bearing zone' around solar-type stars. How many and which of the planets orbiting their primary would fall within this life-zone depends on the size and radiation-emission of the star. In our planetary system the 'life-zone' within which life as we know it is theoretically possible could extend from the orbit of Venus to slightly beyond Mars. Admittedly, Venus would be hotter than the Earth, and regions of the distance of Mars and beyond somewhat colder. But the variations are not so extreme as to exclude the possibility of life resembling that on Earth arising there – providing that the three planets have developed in a similar manner. According to the most recent theories of planetary origin and development, their composition – since they originated from the same gas and dust cloud – should be almost identical with that of Earth, and their subsequent evolution should have followed a similar path. Venus is almost a twin of the Earth in size and gravity, and Mars, although smaller, has a gravitational field of sufficient strength to have retained a considerable atmosphere.

However, the three planets have, in fact, been shown to exhibit vast differences. The Venus probes sent by both the United States and the Soviet Union have presented us with a picture of a planet of extreme surface heat – temperatures in the region of hundreds of degrees centigrade. The surface is so hot, in fact, that some experts have said that it probably has a faint glow. These surface temperatures are sufficient to melt the softer metals, and probes soft-landed on the surface have ceased to function almost immediately. It is extremely rare for us to be able to see any surface markings at all on the planet, due to its dense cloud cover, but recent radar echo-sounding techniques suggest that there are at least two long and extremely high mountain chains there. At present the most popular model for this planet is that of a hot, waterless desert swept by tremendous gales originating in a dense atmosphere of carbon dioxide. Any water vapour is concentrated in the upper layers of the atmosphere and is in the form of ice crystals. This extreme difference between the cold of Venus's upper atmosphere and the tremendous heat on the surface is but one of the planet's many mysteries. The surface atmosphere of carbon dioxide appears to make it certain that life, particularly vegetable life, as we know it, does not exist on Venus.

Another model which has been suggested, although there is as yet no concrete evidence from the Venus probes to support it, is that the surface may have a high hydro-carbon content in the shape of petroleum. A large part of the surface may be covered in petroleum oceans.

Measurements of Venus's movements have provided two surprises. One is that the planet's rotation is extremely slow – each day lasts 243 Earth days – and that it rotates in an opposite manner to all the other planets of the Solar System. This retrograde motion is not understood and no suggestions have been put forward by the astronomers to account for it. Venus orbits the sun at a distance of some sixty million miles in 224·7 days.

Mars has also provided us with many surprises in recent years, and almost all the earlier models which have been suggested regarding the Red Planet have been proved completely wrong. It has always been supposed that, of all the worlds within this planetary system apart from our own, Mars was most likely to have developed living organisms, even intelligent ones. The romantic picture was that of an old, desiccated world turning into a ruddy desert, with the famous network of canals representing a last desperate attempt by the Martians to keep their planet alive by channelling water from the polar caps. The truth, it now turns out, is very different.

The polar caps do exist and they are a very prominent feature seen through a telescope, but they are now reckoned to be a thin layer, perhaps only a few inches deep, of carbon dioxide ice. And the Mariner probes have shown that the famous canals are actually chains of enormous craters, giving an illusion of canals only when seen from a great distance. The close-up photographs of the Martian surface taken by the probes have given us our biggest surprises, as they show a surface incredibly ravaged by enormous craters, deep fissures extending for hundreds of miles, and marks, which, by their configuration, suggest dried-up watercourses or riverbeds. Instrumentation has suggested that the Martian atmosphere has a density only a thousandth of that of Earth, and is mainly carbon dioxide with only minute traces of oxygen or water vapour. Yet this tenuous atmosphere appears able to raise vast dust storms which last for many weeks and cover enormous areas of the surface. Mars orbits the Sun at a distance of 141 million miles, taking 687 days to complete.

Why these two planets should prove so strikingly different from the Earth is something of a mystery which has not yet been resolved. Immanuel Velikovsky, in his book *Worlds in Collision* provided at least one theoretical answer, but this brought down a storm of protest on his head from established scientific opinion; and the theory suffers from one major flaw.

Velikovsky's theory is that the planet Jupiter ejected a mass of material which entered the inner regions of the Solar System as a comet, travelling in a elliptical orbit which brought it into close proximity with the Earth on several occasions. The first, according to Velikovsky, was about 1500 BC, causing, among others, the phenomena noted in Exodus – the plagues and the parting of the Red Sea. The gravitational pull of the comet caused vast upheavals, earthquakes and tidal waves on a huge and global scale. The comet returned several months later causing further destruction, and part of its mass rained down upon the Earth as fire and sticky vapour. This, according to the theory, is how petroleum originated. After several further near-collisions, the comet collided with the planet Mars, interrupting its orbit, and causing it to approach near to the Earth several times, causing further destruction. The Moon's orbit too was interfered with and its distance from the Earth and orbit were changed several times. Eventually the comet lost its tail and became the planet Venus, finally stabilising its orbit, and the other planets and moons also gradually settled down into regular paths once more. Velikovsky places all these events between the third and second millennia BC, that is fairly recent and certainly historic times.

There are many objections to Velikovsky's theories, which we will not dwell on at length, as an exhaustive study on this subject was undertaken in *Colony: Earth.* But the main objection is that comets are extremely tenuous things: 'the nearest one can get to a vacuum and still have a visible object', as it has been said. For a comet to be substantial enough to have condensed into a planet the mass of Venus, it would have had to be so large that it would have covered the entire sky, and possibly been many times the size of the entire Solar System. No phenomenon of such a nature has ever been noted in the annals of ancient times – if it had taken place it is certain that some astronomers, particularly in China and Babylonia, would have made a great many notes for the benefit of posterity.

However, Dr Velikovsky did make some predictions which have proved to be remarkably accurate. Some of his hypotheses regarding the composition of the inner planets concerned in his theory (which was formulated in 1950) have subsequently been partially verified by the discoveries of the space probes.

He predicted a high surface temperature for Venus – not too unlikely, considering that Venus is much nearer to the Sun than the Earth (26 million miles), and it has a thick, heat-retaining atmosphere; and also that Venus would be rich in hydro-carbons. As we have seen, astronomers have since suggested that Venus may possess seas of hydro-carbons – virtually petroleum oceans! – Velikovsky also suggested that Venus had a retrograde axial spin, east to west, instead of west to east, unlike the other planets of the Solar System. He also said that this rotation would be extremely slow, and so it has proved.

He predicted that Mars, far from being a flattish desert criss-crossed by shallow canals or channels, would be scored and fissured with huge craters and cracks caused by the battering the planet had received, and it certainly does bear such marks.

Finally, he said that the Moon would be subject to quakes, and that any future astronauts from Earth would have to be prepared to experience Moonquakes. These do in fact occur, but they are so slight that they can only be detected by instruments.

It seems on the other hand fairly certain that Dr Velikovsky is wrong in several other respects. His time-scale is in error – the effects in Exodus he ascribes to the actions of the comet are now known to have been caused by the great volcanic eruption of Thera (Santorini) in the Eastern Mediterranean. It seems that he may have telescoped a differing series of events into one, because he appears to equate the Exodus phenomena with legends from other parts of the world which would seem to be better connected with the more ancient Flood mythology. It is obvious that the Flood took place a long period of time before the Exodus episode.

Also, gravitational forces of the kind he describes would have shattered completely at least one of the planets involved, probably the smallest, which is Mars.

It has been calculated that the Moon, if it were to spiral closer to the Earth, could not crash into this planet. When it reached a certain point, known as Roche's Limit, gravitational forces would shatter it. Some of the pieces would fall to Earth, causing immense damage, but a greater part of the Moon's debris would adopt a new orbit, and we would then have a ring system similar to that possessed by Saturn. It has been suggested that it is possible that the Saturnian ring system may have formed in this manner.

Notwithstanding the objections to Dr Velikovsky's theory, there remains nevertheless the problem of the peculiarities of the inner planets, and it could be that the only logical solution to this problem is that they were brought about by a catastrophe within the Solar System. What could the nature of such a catastrophe have been? If it was not the fault of a comet, and we cannot see comets posing such a menace, then we must look elsewhere, and it is possible that the solution lies in the asteroid belt. The asteroid belt is a huge mass of debris which lies between the orbits of Mars and Jupiter, and consists of thousands of irregular masses of rocky substance, some of which are almost as large as Mars' tiny moons, and others of which are only a few yards across.

On occasion, some of these asteroids, as they are called, pass fairly close to the Earth, one, called Eros, passing on occasion within several million miles. The meteors which bombard the Earth's atmosphere, some of which are large enough to reach the surface as meteorites, have their origin within the asteroid belt.

There is considerable controversy in scientific circles regarding the origin and nature of the asteroid belt. One school of thought has it that this is the remains of the material left over from the original gas and dust cloud that condensed into the Solar System. The residue was unable to condense into a planetary body because of the close proximity of the gravity field of the giant planet Jupiter, so it forever orbits the Sun as a loose conglomeration of particles. However, many of the asteroids are irregular in shape, and it may be thought that even though a planetary mass could not form, the particles, being dust and gas, would form small masses which would be regular in shape.

The other body of opinion states that the asteroid belt is the remains of a planet which used to orbit between Mars and Jupiter and was for some reason shattered. This event is assumed to have happened many millions of years ago, possibly during Earth's Mesozoic period.

The reason for the dispute is centred around those visitors from the asteroid belt which have from time to time landed on Earth – the meteorites. Several of these have been of such a composition as to suggest that they were formed within a planetary body of some considerable size.

For example, there is the Orgueil meteorite which caused a great deal of controversy, and in fact still does, when the subject is raised. This is said to contain 'organised elements' which, under microscope, appear to resemble fossilised microscopic life forms.

Others have been found to contain diamonds, which can only be formed naturally under great heat and pressure, and this too points to their formation within a planetary body.

A fragment of a coral substance fell from the sky and was collected by an American, Donald Bunce. If it was terrestrial coral, it could, possibly, have fallen from an aircraft. If not – did it perhaps come from the asteroid belt, encased within a mass of stone which disintegrated on its path through the atmosphere, but left the coral intact? Coral, we know, is a product of marine animals, and *if* this came from the asteroid belt, it points not only to a planet destroyed, but to a planet which had once borne life, and moreover where the temperatures must have been high enough to have supported tropical or subtropical forms of life. It would be of a piece with the meteorite containing the mysterious fossilised micro-organisms.

If a planet had orbited between Mars and Jupiter, what could have shattered it? Astronomers consider that there are no known *natural* forces which could disrupt a planet of any size.

There is one theory involving a *natural* catastrophe: that an intruder body of considerable size came into close proximity to the hypothetical planet, so that gravitational forces of the kind already described come into play, with the effect that the planet was torn apart. As there are no traces of such an intrusive body within this system, we must assume that both bodies were shattered by gravitational stress. But there are two objections to this particular theory. One is that it appears extremely unlikely that there are bodies in space just floating between the stars – all stellar objects we have detected would seem to be in association with each other due to gravitational attraction, and as the Galaxy as a whole rotates in a whirlpool fashion, it is extremely unlikely that any stellar object would be able to deviate from the Galactic spin. We have mentioned this factor in connection with the hypothesis of the wandering star colliding with the Sun, thus causing the creation of the planetary system. Many novae and supernovae have been observed during the past several thousand years, but we have never observed colliding stars or planets (although colliding *galaxies are not unknown*). Such a collision would seem to be particularly unlikely in a thinly populated region of space such as the Sun occupies, compared with the more central regions where the stars are clustered closely together.

Second, if the asteroid belt were the remains of *two* planets, or even of a planet and a large moon, it is doubtful whether the mass of either of them could even have been sufficient to comprise a planet large enough to support life or produce diamonds from its interior.

However, the idea that the asteroid belt is the remains of a planet orbiting between Mars and Jupiter has some merit, and it would be one answer to some of the peculiarities we find within the inner planets of the Solar System.

Let us imagine that such a hypothetical planet had shattered, in the position now occupied by the asteroid belt. The nearest other world to this catastrophic event would be Mars, which would be expected to bear the full brunt of the debris scattered in all directions from the explosion. We could therefore expect the surface of Mars to be severely scarred. The impact of masses of rocky debris would produce huge craters, larger than anything we see on the Moon; and the gravitational disturbance caused by the disruption of a planetary body in close proximity could cause a disturbance in the planet's orbit, which, although slight, would have a devastating effect, causing vast earthquakes on the Martian surface. In fact, Mars has proved to be a planet hideously scarred by enormous craters, many of them larger than the Lunar craters; and its surface does contain great cracks and fissures extending for hundreds of miles.

Next in distance from Mars we have the Earth–Moon system. Both of these bodies would experience a rain of debris, and the Moon, being airless, would have less shielding from these missiles than the Earth, so that it too would be heavily cratered. This, of course, is the case. And this proposition connects with an aspect of Moon theory that I have always found questionable. If, as many astronomers believe, the craters on the Moon are impact craters, why is it that no recent craters have appeared? We know, of course, that over many millions of years the Moon could gradually have taken on its present appearance by a slow and continuous bombardment from the asteroid belt. But surely, in the hundreds of years that the Moon has been observed, at least one impact of considerable size should have been seen? The Earth is subject to a ceaseless bombardment of meteoric material, some of which must have been of considerable size to have reached the Earth's surface in sizeable chunks – since most of their mass is vaporised by passage through our dense atmospheric envelope. In the case of the Moon, there being no atmosphere, one would expect many sizeable bolides to strike the lunar surface, gouging out craters at least large enough to be seen through our powerful telescopes.

What has never been pointed out, is that a meteoric object orbiting in space in the normal way and approaching the Earth–Moon system, would surely be most likely to strike the Earth, as the gravitational attraction of the Earth is so much greater than that of the Moon. So if the enormous number of craters on the Moon *are* due to meteoric impact, then there should be traces of many more on Earth. They would be less easy to detect over time, of course, since on

Earth erosion by climate, earthquakes, vegetation, etc., would tend almost to obliterate them.

At present there are known some twelve large craters which are thought to be connected with meteoric collisions. There are a further thirty-two sites which may possibly be the remains of impact craters. The largest of the meteoric craters is the Barringer crater in Arizona, which is some 4,200 feet in diameter and 570 feet deep. The rim is some 160 feet above the floor of the plain. No traces of a large meteorite have been found in the vicinity of the crater, however, and digging below the floor of the crater has failed to produce any remains. But prior to 1902 many nickel-iron specimens were collected from the vicinity of the crater, which tends to support the meteoric impact theory, as many meteorites are composed of nickel iron.

It may seem reasonable to assume that the explosion of a planet orbiting beyond Mars would account for the cratering of Mars, the Moon, and to a lesser extent, the Earth. The fragments flung outwards from the explosion towards the outer regions of the Solar System would scarcely affect the outer planets, the nearest of course being giant Jupiter, which is thought, in any case, to be more gaseous than solid. Even if solid, its great mass would not be much affected by such impacts. As far as can be calculated, the present mass of all the asteroids and meteoric debris in the asteroid belt is some 1/1,000th of the Earth's mass. To judge from the vast number of craters on Mars and the Earth–Moon system, and taking into account also the considerable volume of meteors and meteoric dust assimilated by Earth alone over the centuries, it is not unreasonable to conclude that a mass of planetary dimensions, albeit smaller than Earth and Venus, once existed in the region now occupied by the asteroid belt.

As we have said, many astronomers do not agree that there ever was a planet orbiting between Mars and Jupiter; but some astronomers do have a measure of agreement that the Moon's craters appear to have been formed at one particular point in time, which is why there exist two schools of thought as to their formation. One school favours the impact theory, whereas the other considers that the craters were formed by volcanic action in the Moon's early stage of evolution. However, in view of the numerous craters on Mars, where there exists the possibility that they were formed long after the planet had ceased to evolve, and the fact that craters similar to those of the Moon exist on Earth in areas where there is no trace of vulcanism, the impact theory on the whole seems more likely.

If, then, the craters on the Moon, Mars and Earth were formed at a particular point in time, then there must have been a prior cause, and that cause must have been an event of tremendous violence. This cause could have been the explosion of a planetary mass orbiting between Mars and Jupiter. But if this were so, it must have been an explosion of exceptional violence for the fragments to have been flung at great velocities across the millions of miles which separate the present asteroid belt from Mars and the Earth–Moon system.

Astronomers have said that they know of no series of natural events which would lead to the disruption of a planetary mass without the interference of another planetary body. Such an event is only possible when two bodies come into close proximity to each other, and gravitational forces will cause disintegration of one or both of them. What then, if there was only one planetary body involved, was the cause of the explosion? Are we forced to the conclusion that it was artificial? This would presume the activities of an intelligent race, and here we have several possibilities to choose from. Weapons powerful enough to cause an entire planet to explode are unknown to us, but they could possibly have been nuclear devices of immense power, or weapons based upon the control of gravitational fields. We pointed out in *Colony: Earth* that control of gravity would not only be a tool of tremendous value, but also a weapon of awesome power.

Was our hypothetical planet inhabited? If it can be proven that the meteorites do contain fossil material, and that they do originate in the asteroid belt, then it is more than probable that they are the remnants of a destroyed planet which was life-bearing – it would not be too far from the Sun to be so. And where there is life, there is also the possibility of intelligent life.

Was there more than one inhabited planet in this Solar System at some point in the past? We have at least three possibilities. Earth we know to be inhabited. There is the possibility based on the evidence of the meteorites that there was perhaps a life-bearing planet orbiting beyond Mars, and there is Mars itself.

The photographs taken by the Mariner space probes have revealed what look like the beds of dried up watercourses. They have the same meandering appearance with many tributary branches. The probes have also revealed that the Martian atmosphere is extremely tenuous, only 1 per cent of Earth's at surface level, and that it appears to contain no free oxygen. This has surprised our scientists, who find the lack of atmosphere difficult to account for. It has been suggested that in the past Mars may have had a considerable atmosphere. If some of the surface markings really are the remains of watercourses then there must have been a considerable amount of surface water and, presumably, an atmosphere not too dissimilar to Earth's. What, then, has happened? One possible solution put forward by the scientists is connected with the fact that the Mariner spacecraft were unable to detect an appreciable magnetic field on Mars, suggesting that the original iron content of the planet did not sink towards the centre, as in the case of Earth, but remained on the surface. Water vapour in the atmosphere is separated by the action of ultra-violet light into oxygen and hydrogen. Hydrogen, the lighter gas, could escape into space, and the oxygen would then combine with the iron, forming a rust compound. This theory would account for the ruddy appearance of Mars. However, this is only a tentative answer and the elimination of the atmosphere may have taken a more violent form.

If we had three inhabited planets within the Solar System and a conflict arose between the intelligent inhabitants, it is possible that one planet was completely destroyed, and that Mars was so severely damaged by the debris and the use of highly destructive weapons that its atmosphere was vaporised. Perhaps the War in Heaven mentioned in the ancient annals was a conflict between warring worlds.

We have suggested that man may be of extra-terrestrial

origin, and have postulated that vehicles from other Solar Systems once in a remote age surveyed this system looking for planets suitable for life. It is possible that they found not one but three planets suitable for life, or perhaps already bearing life of some kind. Perhaps both Mars and Earth, and possibly Venus, were occupied, and the outer and now destroyed planet was originally used as a defensive installation. We are considering using the Moon for human occupation; we may also consider building missile installations there in order to use the Moon as an impregnable military base which could threaten any part of the Earth. So it is possible that something of the sort was carried out in the remote past. In another chapter we shall deal with the possibility that space travel, and also possibly interstellar travel, was known to the ancients.

We have considered the possibility of a nuclear conflict on Earth in the distant past; we should perhaps also consider whether this possibility was limited to Earth, or was carried to other worlds.

A past civilisation which had developed nuclear weapons and missiles would doubtless also have developed space travel, even if only of a rudimentary kind; this is the stage at which we have now arrived. Possibly if they had made their discoveries in a different order, they may have perfected space travel first. Perhaps they built military installations on the Moon and elsewhere.

It is very curious, and came as a complete surprise to the astronauts and to our scientists, that the Moon is apparently covered in 'glass'. There have been discovered a vast quantity of small glass spheres on the surface of the Moon, and it has been suggested that these were formed by the high temperatures obtained by the impact of high velocity meteorites. However, the temperatures needed to vitrify rock to this extent are extremely high, as we have seen: would meteorites really strike the Moon's surface with the hyper-velocities necessary? The gravitational attraction of the Moon is only one-fifth that of the Earth, and we have no terrestrial evidence to show that meteoric impact causes this particular phenomenon. With our gravitational field one would expect the velocities to be correspondingly higher, notwithstanding the cushioning effect of our atmosphere. The frictional effect of the passage through atmosphere, thus initially raising the temperature of the meteorite high enough to melt a considerable proportion of it, should surely create much higher temperatures. On the face of it, it does seem more likely that a meteorite, striking cold surface rocks in a cold state – there being no atmosphere on the Moon either to impede its passage or raise its temperature by friction – would merely cause pulverisation. Indeed, it has been thought that the layer of fine dust which covers the surface of the Moon is caused in part by the eroding away of the surface material by the great contrast in temperatures between night and day on the Moon, and in part by the pulverisation of meteoric material. If this pulverisation of meteoric material is one of the reasons for the Moon's dusty layer, then it can hardly be responsible for the glassy spherules, for which extremely high temperatures are required.

There are also areas of glasslike material, which may remind us of the vitrified areas which exist on Earth, particularly in present-day desert areas, and show a marked similarity to vitrification caused by recent nuclear tests in desert regions. Could the similar phenomena on the Moon have had a similar cause – thermo-nuclear heat?

I quote here from *The Solar System* by Frank W. Cousins, Chapter 10 'On the Earth/Moon System'[1]:

The discovery that some parts of the Moon are paved with pieces of glass supports the view that the Moon has suffered impacts of a very energetic nature. The report of these findings in *The Times* of September 2 1969, drew the following letter from Mr D. O'Brien of Gonville and Caius College, Cambridge:

Sir: It is satisfying to read your report today that the Moon is made largely of glass. This is just what Empedocles in the fifth century before Christ said it was made of.

From where did this Greek obtain his truly remarkable information? Was it guesswork, assuming it would need a

1. John Baker, 1972, page 177.

glassy surface to make it shine so brightly by reflected sun-light? Did he know that the Moon shone by reflected light? Even if he did, was this the reason? Perhaps he had access to more ancient *knowledge*. We shall, at a later stage, examine some areas of astronomical knowledge from ancient times which it does not seem possible could have been obtained by naked-eye observation alone.

Still bearing in mind the Lunar glasses being formed by temperatures of the range created by thermo-nuclear re-actions, we turn our attention to some mysterious objects found in certain areas of the Earth, which are reckoned to have an extra-terrestrial origin, possibly on the Moon. These objects are known as tektites. They are a silica-rich obsidian glass different from terrestrial obsidian, and the greatest number have been found in Australia, Indo-China, the Philippines and Moldavia. They are usually jet-black and take the form of button shapes, spheres and dumb-bells. It is believed (Baker) that they are extra-terrestrial in origin, and have gained their shapes by aerodynamic ablation through high-speed flight and kinetic heating on their passage through the Earth's atmosphere.

Chapman (*Nature* 188, 333, 1960) is of the opinion that they have originated on the Moon, but this view is not universally accepted and their origin is still uncertain.

Urey has suggested that they may have originated in a cometary collision with the Earth. He therefore proposes that they are after all terrestrial in nature, and produced by extremely high temperatures almost instantaneously. He likens the explosive heat to that produced by a high-altitude burst of a hydrogen bomb. They represent, in other words, a 'flash burn' effect. If the effect which produces tektits is com-parable with a nuclear explosion, then perhaps this is how they were in fact produced. We have a certain amount of evidence to suggest that nuclear weapons were used on Earth in the past, although modern nuclear weapons have failed to produce tektites. Did they result from a nuclear explosion on the Moon, or from similar explosions which may have been responsible for the destruction of a planet orbiting be-yond Mars? The difference between the vitrified areas on Earth and the Moon, and the Moon 'marbles' may lie largely in the fact that these particular objects were subjected to high-velocity flight through the Earth's atmosphere.

It is not impossible that tektites have the same origin as meteorites, and represent fragments of the vitrified areas of a planet shattered by nuclear explosions of great power.

The destruction of a planet beyond Mars could thus furnish us with an explanation for the appearance of Mars and the Moon, and explain some of the craters on Earth. When this event took place it is difficult to say. Most astronomers who favour the theory that the asteroid belt is the remains of a planet place the event many millions of years in the past, but this may not necessarily be so. The event could have happened only some thousands of years ago, and be related to the legendary War in Heaven. It is interesting to observe here part of the legend regarding the reason for the construction of the Great Pyramid:

> King Saurid, son of Salahoc, reigned in Egypt three hundred years before the Flood and dreamt one night that Earth was convulsed; all the houses fell down upon men and the stars collided in the heavens such that their pieces covered the sun. The King awoke in terror, rushed into the Sun Temple and consulted the priests and diviners. Akliman, the wisest of them, said he too had had a similar dream ... it was then that the King had the pyramids built in that angular way suitable for withstanding *even the blows from stars* ... (Italics mine, Author.)

Blows from stars – could this be the event we have described as possible – the destruction of a planet and the bombardment of its fragments? If so, this would place the event within the last 10,000 years. We can date the age of the rocks which compose asteroidal meteorites, but we cannot so easily date the time when they came to be in their present fragmentary state.

This, of course, does not solve the riddle of the other inner planet of the Solar System, Venus. It may be that Venus, provided it was then following its present path, orbits too far from the centre of the explosion to be affected.

Velikovsky, in *Worlds in Collision*, says that at one time Venus did not occupy the prominent place it occupies today – this position in the eyes of the ancients was occupied by Jupiter. Venus is such a bright object that it seems somewhat surprising that it should not have occupied a prominent place in ancient observational astronomy after the Sun and the Moon. It is far brighter than Jupiter. Either there was a time when Venus did not possess its dense atmosphere and therefore lacked its high albido, or it orbited much further from the Sun.

We see the Solar System as it has been known for the past several thousand years, and so our astronomers have the firm opinion that this is how it has been for countless millions of years. This view may not necessarily be correct. There could have been great changes in the system due to catastrophic events of which we are not aware, and which have left no observational traces. Because the system has been stable for the six thousand years for which we possess written records, it should not be automatically assumed that this is how things have always been.

It is possible that when we are able to undertake human exploration of the inner planets, we may be able to answer some of these riddles. Already our first tentative explorations of the Moon have provided many surprises, some of them at variance with our previous observational evidence.

Possibly the surprises which await us on the surface of Mars and Venus will be even greater than those we have encountered on the Moon.

7

Ancient Astronomy

A re-examination of ancient scientific thought and writings leads to the conclusion that science has a much longer history than has been thought, and that much of what we think of today as discovery for the first time is only re-discovery of ancient and half-forgotten knowledge. It appears also to be true that the more ancient the source, the more knowledge of a basic and profound nature existed. This, like our evidence on the origins of civilisation itself, is the reverse of what we would predict if the first dawn of civilisation were at Egypt and Sumer.

Knowledge existing in antiquity regarding astronomy provides us with many surprises. Most authorities give us the impression that astronomy in antiquity was limited to what was observable by the naked eye, then frequently falsely interpreted and connected with superstition and astrology. This is true enough of many aspects of later Babylonian, Egyptian and early Greek thought, which shows us a simplified and often totally erroneous picture of the Universe. A flat Earth, with the sky a solid dome with holes in it to cause the appearance of stars, the Earth held up by a turtle swimming in the primeval ocean, the Earth held on the back of an elephant, Atlas holding up the sky and many other fanciful ideas seem absurd today; but there were older ideas which were more in line with present day knowledge. Even in the Middle Ages, knowledge of the Universe was extremely limited, and the idea that the Earth revolved round the Sun was held to be ridiculous – the Earth was fixed at the centre of the Universe, and everything revolved around it.

For the past several hundred years almost everyone has known, for example, that the Earth is a sphere (there is still, even today, a small Flat Earth Society), although throughout Medieval Europe everyone was taught that the Earth was flat – it was heresy, and rather dangerous, to think other-wise. Even today, in an advanced country like England, it is surprising how vague astronomical truths are to the majority of people. Many people, for example, thought that the first Lunar astronauts would somehow fall off if they weren't careful, and others thought that this line of experimentation would interfere with the terrestrial weather. I have heard such comments made myself. This, in an enlightened country in the latter part of the twentieth century. It is hardly sur-prising therefore that earlier people from non-technological societies should have had an even more difficult time grasp-ing astronomical realities, and even the literate and educated folk of the time did not understand. Little wonder that the knowledge stemming from the remote past was either not understood or ignored, or dismissed by the then leaders of thought, be it scientific or religious.

Thousands of years ago it was known that the Earth was a sphere and that it hung, unsupported, in space. This fact is even mentioned in the Bible – 'The Earth hangs in nothing-ness' it says – something which appears to have been ignored for most of the lifetime of Christianity. It appears that even Christian societies believed what they wanted to believe and ignored the rest. Many ancient thinkers were aware of the true shape of the Earth.

'The Earth is round and it revolves around the Sun,' said Anaximander (610–547 BC). Pythagoras said in the sixth cen-tury BC that the Earth is a globe.

King Chandragupta told the Greek ambassador Megas-thenes in 302 BC: 'Our brahmins believe the Earth to be a sphere.'

Many ancient thinkers not only knew that the Earth was a globe, but they estimated its size, its orbit and axial rotation.

Aristarchus of the third century BC says: 'The Earth re-volves in an oblique circle while it rotates at the same time about its own axis.'

'The Earth spins on its axis once in twenty-four hours,' said Heraclides of Pontus in the fourth century BC.

Eratosthenes measured both the circumference of the Earth and its diameter. There is a discrepancy of only 80 km between the figure he obtained for the polar diameter and that shown by modern astronomers.

The Sanskrit book Surya Siddhanta contains fairly accurate calculations of the diameter of the Earth and its distance from the Moon.

Chang Heng of China (AD 78–139) said the Earth is an egg, and that its axis points to the Pole Star.

In more modern times, Columbus made a study of all available classical sources before embarking on his voyage of discovery to the New World, and in a letter preserved in Madrid he made the remarkable statement that the Earth was slightly *pear shaped*. It is only in the last ten years that space satellites have revealed this fact to us. It was previously quite unknown to our astronomers. From what ancient and since untraced text did he discover this information?

Parmedides of the sixth century BC says, about the Moon: 'It illuminates the night with borrowed light' – an obvious reference to the fact that the Moon is illuminated by reflected sunlight.

Empedocles (494–434 BC): 'The Moon circles round the Earth – a borrowed light.'

We have already mentioned the Sanskrit legend about the Lunar Pitris and the great age of the Moon, and it is not only in India that the Moon was regarded as being older than the Earth. In Mayan art the Moon is represented as an old man with a conch shell. The Moon Goddess Ixchel of Mexico was known as the Grandmother. In the religion of many primitive peoples, the Moon is considered the first man who died, the Encyclopaedia Britannica says.

It is only since our astronauts landed on the Moon that we have learned that the Moon is indeed older than the Earth, and that its composition is different from that of this planet.

The most extraordinary astronomical calculations were made by the astronomers of the Mayan civilisation of Central America. The astronomers estimated the Lunar month as 29·53020 days, and the Palanque astronomers as 29·53086. According to our astronomers the period is 29·53059 days, midway between the Palanque and Copan calculations of the ancient Mayas.

Moving away from the Earth–Moon system, even more

extraordinary facts have come to light about ancient astronomy. There are Babylonian inscriptions which mention the Horns of Ishtar (Venus) which refer to the crescent shape of the planet. The 'horns' of Venus can only be seen through a telescope.

Babylonian priests recorded their observations of the four greater satellites of Jupiter – and they cannot be seen without the aid of a telescope. Prof G. Rawlinson says: 'There is said to be distinct evidence that they observed the four satellites of Jupiter and strong reason for belief that they were acquainted likewise with the seven satellites of Saturn.'

The Dogons of Sudan have a curious legend about the 'dark companion of Sirius'. The dim companion star of Sirius can only be seen through the most powerful of our present telescopes, such as the 200-inch of Palomar. Also the Dogons say there are three stars, one of which, brighter than iron, is so heavy that a tiny grain would weigh more than 480 donkey loads. We have calculated that Sirius B's density is fifty times that of water and a small box would weigh a ton. There is a suspected third star.

Democritus of Greece in the fifth century BC says: 'Space is filled with myriads of stars and the Milky Way is but a vast conglomeration of distant suns.'

Aristarchus said that the distance which separates us from the stars is immeasurable.

How did these ancient Greeks know this? It is curious that the ancients spoke of looking at the sky and distant objects 'through tubes'. Telescopes in antiquity?

Heraclitus (540–475 BC) thought that each star was the centre of a planetary system. Democritus said that other worlds come into being and die. Only some of the worlds of other stars are suitable for life. Anaxagoras (500–428 BC) wrote: 'Other earths produce the necessary sustenance for inhabitants.'

The Vedas of India speak of life on other celestial bodies far from the Earth.

On comets: 'Comets move in orbits like the planets,' writes Seneca. Aristotle remembered the Pythagoreans who taught that comets were stellar bodies which appeared after long periods of time.

Our present ideas of the formation of the Solar System out of a flattened disc of gas and dust was anticipated in ancient times. The Maya Popol Vuh says: 'Like the mist, like a cloud, and like a cloud of dust was the creation.'

The Huai T'zu book and the Lun Heng writted by Wang Chung (AD 82) stated that worlds were made out of whirl-pools of primary matter.

We are all familiar with the signs of the Zodiac, and the names which have been given to the constellations. Orion, Taurus, Aquarius, Pisces, etc., are well known; but it takes a good stretching of the imagination to see these stellar groups taking on the appearance of the descriptions that have been given to them – an Ox, Hunter, Water Carrier, etc. It seems all the more surprising, therefore, that many different cultures from all over the world have the same names for the constellations. One may have thought that various cultures would have interpreted these star groups differently, and invented descriptive or fanciful names very different from each other. Such is not the case.

Orion, the Hunter of the Middle East, is known as the Hunter of the Autumn Hunt in China.

The Western Aquarius is echoed by Tlaloc, the Rain God of Mexico – both connected with water.

The Babylonian sign of the Ram is the Sheep in China.

The Chinese Ox constellation is Taurus (the Bull) in the West.

Giorgio de Santillana, in *The Origins of Scientific Thought*: 'They were repeated without question substantially the same from Mexico to Africa and Polynesia – and have remained with us to this day.'

Tomas, in his book *We Are Not The First*, has suggested that early civilisations may have had access to older lists of constellations which they used to identify the stars.

All these things we have mentioned would seem to point to there having been a greater knowledge of observational astronomy in the past than has usually been realised, and even also a knowledge of astro-physics, to judge from the Dogons and their mention of Sirius. Some of the knowledge which existed could not have been obtained without instrumentation. The moons of Jupiter and Saturn cannot be seen without the use of telescopes, and it goes without saying that the dim companion of Sirius cannot be seen without the aid of a very powerful and sophisticated telescope. We have not been able to find traces of telescopes from the remote past, although small lenses capable of slight magnification have been found in Mesopotamia, which shows that a knowledge of optics did exist.

How did the Maya arrive at their accurate computations regarding the Lunar month? Such minute fractions of a day cannot be obtained without precise and accurate instrumentation. As far as we are aware, the Maya possessed no such instruments – this civilisation hardly ever even used metals. There is what appears to be an astronomical observatory at Chichen Itza in Yucatan – the shape is almost identical to modern observatories, minus the scientific equipment. Did such a place once hold astronomical devices – or was it merely a model, a copy of such a place? Were the Mayas merely copying a structure from an earlier, vanished era, knowing its connection with the heavens, but either unaware of the equipment it should house or unable to construct it properly, so that the building was unable to fulfil its true function? Perhaps they were fulfilling a sacred task, in the same way that the Brahmins faithfully copied the mathematics of a vanished science, because it was a sacred duty, and therefore the act was (to them) an act of homage to the gods. Did the Mayas actually make these calculations of the Lunar month, or did they have the information transmitted down to them from a vanished scientific era? This again could be a close parallel to the Brahmins.

We know that a certain amount of knowledge of observational astronomy has survived from an ancient period, some of which can only have been obtained with the aid of advanced instrumentation. This presupposes a legacy from an advanced scientific era of which no trace remains. If such an advanced scientific society existed with the devices of astronomical instrumentation, then there should also have existed some knowledge, not only of observational astronomy, but also of astro-physics. Very little evidence of this does in fact exist, but there is some, which should make us pause. The ancients were aware of some things outside of their Earth-

bound state, which, properly speaking, they should not have
known – unless someone, at some time in the past, had actually experienced them. This is not to say that an ancient
Sumerian or Babylonian had experience of space personally,
but that he may have had traditions or documentary evidence to draw upon which have survived in writings.

The Babylonian Epic of Etana, written 4,700 years ago,
has drawn comments in recent times because it presents a
picture of the Earth seen from a great height, and possibly
from space, which, because of its accuracy, could not have
been based on guesswork. The Flight of Etana says:

'I will take you to the throne of Anu,' said the eagle.
They had soared for an hour and then the eagle said:
'Look down, what has become of Earth!' Etana looked
down and saw that the Earth had become like a hill and
the sea like a well. And so they flew for another hour, and
once again Etana looked down; the Earth was now like a
grinding stone and the sea like a pot. After the third hour
the Earth was only a speck of dust, and the sea no longer
seen.

Anu, the Great God of the Babylonians, was god of the
Heavenly Great Depths – which we today call Space.

The cosmology of the later ages of Babylon – which made
the Earth the centre of the Universe, around which all the
stars were fixed – would never have given rise to the concept
that the Earth could shrink through distance to the size of a
speck. The idea could not have been imagined. But more
ancient times had a more accurate view.

The infinite reaches of space are accurately described in
the Egyptian Book of the Dead: 'This place has no air, its
depth is unfathomable and it is as black as the blackest
night.'

It was in the time of the Chinese Emperor Yao that a
great disaster overtook the Earth: the seas rose and covered
all the land, there were plagues of fire and great earthquakes.
This Emperor had an engineer called Chih-Chiang-Tzu-Yu
who voyaged to the Moon on a celestial bird. This bird advised him the times of the rising and setting of the sun. He

travelled by mounting currents of luminous air. Once in space, the Chinese astronaut 'did not perceive the rotary movement of the Sun'. On the Moon, he saw the 'frozen-looking horizon'. It appears that on one occasion his wife Chang Ngo flew to the Moon, 'a luminous sphere, shining like glass, of enormous size and very cold'.

There are some statements in this passage which take the story out of the realm of fairy tale. The celestial bird gave him directions – was this information from a computer, of a nature similar to that obtained by present-day astronauts? The currents of luminous air could refer to the fiery jets of a rocket propulsion motor. Again, we have a parallel to the ancient Greek statement about the glassy appearance of the Moon, which we have found to be true – and only discovered *since men set foot on the Moon*.

An ancient Sanskrit text, the Surya Siddhanta, makes mention of Siddhas and Vidyaharas (philosophers and scientists) who examined the Earth 'below the Moon but above the clouds'. This could relate to scientific surveys undertaken in something like our present-day orbiting space laboratories. This is an extremely interesting point, because there are certain ancient maps in existence containing information apparently unobtainable before modern times. The Antarctic map of Piri Reis, for example, shows the Antarctic and South American continent and is said to date from before the time of Alexander the Great. What is more, there is a distortion on this map which exactly fits the shape of South America when seen from a satellite orbiting *at a height of some seventy miles*. Was it from an orbiting space station of the type described in the Sanskrit text that the original of this map was made?

The Samaranagana Sutradhara, also from India, speaks of a time when men flew in the air and *heavenly beings* came down from the sky.

Prof H. L. Harriyappa of Mysore University wrote that in a remote period 'gods came to the Earth often, and some men visited the immortals in heaven'.

The Mahabharata – the now famous text which mentions nuclear weapons – says, in its fifth volume: 'Infinite is the space populated by the perfect ones and gods, there is no limit to their delightful abodes.'

In an ancient Chinese book, the Shi Ching, the Divine Emperor saw the crime and vice arising on the Earth (do we not have echoes of Genesis here?) and commanded Chong and Li to cease communication between the Earth and sky 'and since then there has been no more going up and down'.

In the Royal Pedigree of Tibetan Kings, it is said that the first Seven Kings came from the stars, and were able to 'walk in the sky'.

What are we to make of all these extraordinary statements connected with astronomy and cosmology in ancient texts? Some are connected with astronomical knowledge of an advanced type unobtainable without instrumentation, other information could only possibly have been obtained by flights in space, and there are references to actual travel in space, both by terrestrials and by visitors from the stars.

First, let us consider the observational astronomical knowledge of the Greeks and Babylonians. From where did they obtain their knowledge in the first instance? Some of the statements by the Greek thinkers may have been educated guesses, but on the other hand, they are invariably so accurate, so did they have a source of information in more ancient writings?

The cradle of knowledge of ancient Greece, and this is also possibly true of Babylonia, was Egypt. Greek thinkers and students went in unknown numbers to the wisdom of Egypt for their learning. There was a great University in Alexandria with a library of 700,000 books in scroll form. The Bruchion contained 400,000 books and the Serapeum 300,000. The facilities at the University complex also included medicine, mathematics, astronomy, an observatory, botanical and zoological gardens, and the place could cater for 14,000 students. The university and library were razed to the ground during Julius Caesar's Egyptian campaign. The library was supposed to contain the history and knowledge of the human race.

Was this where the sages of Greece obtained some of their knowledge and ideas of astronomy? Where did the Egyptian priests and men of wisdom obtain all these books and all the knowledge they contained?

We have perhaps a clue from legend about the true function and purpose of the Great Pyramids. In the myth, a King Saurid, whom we have already mentioned, was warned in a dream that there was to be a great flood, and he was advised to build a great Pyramid to store *all the world's knowledge*. According to this, the pyramids were not built as tombs, but as shelters, not specifically for people, but to store knowledge within. It is known that the pyramids were built by a technique which cannot be duplicated today – for all our technological achievements we would be unable to build the Great Pyramid of Cheops. If we assume that the pyramid-builders were representatives of an advanced civilisation aware of a great catastrophe about to overtake them, then it is possible that they secreted this knowledge of the sciences within the pyramid, to be brought forth when the danger was past. It is this knowledge which was the basis of the Alexandrian library.

We shall never know the extent of the loss to humanity of this library – if the knowledge that has been handed down to us by the Greeks is but a minute fraction of what they remembered or recorded from their studies in Egypt, the loss is probably incalculable. Possibly there was more knowledge of the sciences contained in this one library alone than all we have so painfully gathered during the past two and a half centuries. The Alexandria library was not the only one in Egypt – the documents in the library of the Temple of Ptah at Memphis were also totally destroyed.

As we have seen, there are some things which could only have been discovered by actual exploration, such as the knowledge that glass exists on the Moon. We have only discovered this fact by going there – it now seems within the realms of possibility that these space flights may not be the first ones men from this planet have made. Have men trodden before on the surface of the Moon from a former civilisation which has been forgotten?

The ancients mention that other stars have planets – how could they possibly have said this unless such a fact had been known at some time in the past? It is only within the last several decades that our astronomers have come to the conclusion that possibly all solar-type stars possess planetary systems. It is now thought that there must be millions of planetary systems in the Galaxy, and therefore thousands of Earth-type worlds. This is what the ancients have said; statements ignored and dismissed as fairy tales are now being verified by our scientists!

How much else of what the ancients have written is true? That men visited other worlds in the past and that heavenly beings – these must be the inhabitants of other planets – came to Earth. The old legends are clear that men understood the nature of the space that exists between the worlds. This knowledge could best be gained by experiencing the reality of these gulfs, and the writings do indeed seem to be based on these experiences rather than on theoretical speculation.

A highly advanced civilisation of the past which had space travel, and perhaps travel to the stars, may have had contact with other cultures in space. The theories we have advanced that mankind on Earth may have been an offshoot of a galactic civilisation would mean that such contacts were feasible. It is also possible that there existed channels of communication between the civilisation here and civilisations elsewhere in the Galaxy. It could be wondered – whether this fact of communication with advanced cultures in space – in the heavens – is the true origin of prayer? All through history men have prayed to the gods who dwelt – invariably – in the sky. We know that in 'heaven' – 'up there' – is endless space, and other stars and planets. The ancients talked knowingly of other worlds in space, and there are legends of the visits of the heavenly ones to Earth. Today we can infer the existence of planetary systems from the movement of slow-spinning solar-type stars in the near vicinity of our Sun. Prayer, then, may be based, originally, on communication between the inhabitants of this planet and a galactic civilisation. Perhaps the communication was on a telepathic level; we have a certain amount of evidence that telepathy is possible. If telepathy is one of the extra-sensory powers which lie largely dormant now in the human mind, we cannot be sure that this was always so. If these powers are now dormant, it may be that there was a time when they were active, but have atrophied with the passage of time. If it is true that man is a degenerate species, this degeneration would also affect the mind. We also do not know whether telepathy would be subject to the limitations of electro-magnetic radiation: it may be instantaneous over many light years. It is one possible method of communication, which, unlike any form of radio or television transmission, may not be subject to the limitations of the velocity of light, and able therefore to make immediate contact with other beings many light years away.

As the gods are invariably situated in the sky, and the sky is where other worlds exist which may contain intelligent forms of life, then the gods must be the inhabitants of those other worlds. Telepathic communication may be one method of passing information – and perhaps also orders – between man on Earth and the 'gods' in space, and there may be other methods ...

It is interesting in this connection to take account of two factors from mythology which have a bearing on the subject.

One is the curious statement which occurs time and time again that 'time' itself is different from mortals to the gods, and indeed for human beings when they traverse the heavenly gulfs. We have already noted that a Day of Brahma is a vastly longer period of time than a terrestrial day, and we have noted that the same thing applies to the Egyptian Horus. We also find this in the Judaic/Christian tradition, where it is said of God 'that a thousand years are but a moment in thy sight'.

The vision of Isaiah contains a curious story which has a connection with time differences away from the Earth. He was taken to Heaven by an angel to see God. The angel then told him it was time to return to Earth, and Isaiah, surprised, said, 'I have been here but two hours.' To which the angel replied, 'Not two hours but thirty-two years.' Isaiah was grieved to think that such a long journey would mean old age or death, but the angel told him that he would not have aged on his return.

In Exodus we remember Moses went up to the Mount to meet God. A strange cloud came down on the mount with smoke, flame and thunderings, and a loud voice told the people to stand back lest they be killed. Then Moses saw the feet of God standing on a pavement as if of crystal, and was warned not to look at the face of God.

This seems a somewhat curious statement. In modern terms, how could we translate this passage? Was the odd cloud in fact a large space vehicle, perhaps windowless. If it was highly reflective (our lunar vehicles are covered with a highly reflective layer to prevent excessive heat absorption) then it would reflect the clouds and sky and may well appear to the natives to have taken on the appearance of a cloud itself. The flame and thunder could be the exhaust of braking rockets, fatal to approach, as anyone who has observed the ascent of a Saturn rocket would realise. The loud voice could have been broadcast from a loudspeaker. Seeing the feet of God means that what Moses saw was a *person*. It was no amorphous mental entity he saw, but an actual personage standing on a – what? – platform extruded from the ship? Why was he not allowed to see the face of God? Was it perhaps that the 'God' was wearing a helmet with all the attachments of an astronaut, with a visor hiding his features, and did not wish to terrify the primitive any more than necessary? This concept of a god who occupies a certain limited physical space is entirely different from the view of God possessed by modern thinkers, and indeed from the basic religious concepts of deism which have more in common with some aspects of modern scientific thought than with primitive superstition.

The God who has feet and stands is a person, whether or not this person has an extended lifespan to make him seem immortal, and has powers at his command which would seem awesome even to us today. Such an entity could not, by our standards, be regarded as 'God' as we understand the term, and could at last be comprehended by modern scientists, even if not properly understood.

In this connection, we may note that the Mormon sect of Christianity (The Church of Latter Day Saints) are quite convinced, and have as a main tenet of their faith, that God is a person of 'flesh and bones' as they put it, and they even believe that this God has a planetary home in the Galaxy. This idea, which almost seems 'science fiction', is proposed quite seriously, and certainly echoes more ancient concepts of the gods from the sky.

The other curious factor about this God of the Hebrews, in this context, is that he would seem to be aware of events which had happened many thousands of years before. He apparently knew what their ancestors had done. This either means that the God had a lifespan of many thousands of years, or that he was in the same position as Isaiah with his journey to heaven. It may be an effect of time dilation.

This factor of a difference of time in space, as mentioned in the myths, is actually borne out by modern science, and is called time dilation. If a vehicle approaches relativistic velocities (near the speed of light) then time itself appears to slow. It is not that time itself is actually changed, but that the distance travelled shortens, hence the 'time' shrinkage. This means, in effect, that a vehicle travelling at near the speed of light to say the Centadurus system, takes five years to get there and five years on the return voyage. Between the disappearance of the ship and its return again, ten years will have elapsed, *to those awaiting its return on Earth*. To the crew, however, only several weeks will appear to have passed. It has been said that a circumnavigation of the Galaxy at a minute fraction under the speed of light could be accomplished in half a million years *elapsed time*, but could be completed in well under the lifetime of the crew.

We have already mentioned that a voyage to the Pleiades and back would take just under a thousand years, which connects reasonably well both with ancient legends about this star group being the home of the Gods, and the thousand-year interval between visits of the Gods. This means that the God of Israel could make many voyages at thousand-year intervals, covering a span of many thousands of years, and yet the astronaut need hardly age at all. Such a traveller may well have seemed to the ancients not only immortal, but a god!

It certainly seems strange how ancient legends of spatial voyages and modern relativistic theory converge: this must surely be more than a coincidence.

The other factor is the channels of communication with the Gods.

The Phoenician Sanchuniathon (1193 BC) and Philo

Byblos (AD 15) mention animated stones. The Christian historian Eusebius (*circa* AD 260–340) carried such a stone on his chest which answered questions in a low whistling.

The Bible mentions 'teraphim' or images which answered questions. (Ezekiel 21 : 21 and Genesis 31 : 34). Maimodes (1135–1204) in *Les Regeles des Mouers* states : 'The worshippers of the teraphim claimed that as the light of the stars filled the carved statue, it was put in rapport with the intelligences of those distant stars and planets who used the statue as an instrument. It is in this manner that the teraphim taught people many useful arts and sciences.'

Seldenus in Die Diis Syriis mentions teraphims consecrated to a special star or planet and says they were known to the Egyptians.

What were these speaking stones, and stone or crystal devices which could pass messages from the stars? Do they not perhaps remind us of transistors, widely used in radio and TV today and which are crystals? Were they perhaps channels of communication akin to radio for communication with other worlds, or vehicles orbiting invisibly around our planet?

Again, we have a myth which is not quite so mythical when we relate it to modern techniques.

It is becoming less and less a fantasy that in a distant past astronomical knowledge was at a high level; and that it was based both on observation by sophisticated instruments and on the direct experience of space travel and contact with other worlds and intelligent life elsewhere in space. Perhaps one day our astronauts will see other, older footprints in the dust of the Moon, and know that men in a forgotten past also have trodden the road to the stars.

8

The Antiquity of Science

We have observed that there existed in the past a great deal of knowledge about physics and astronomy which could not have been gained without instrumentation and the resources of a technological civilisation. It is suggested that repositories of the knowledge possessed by a superior culture were created when the civilisation was threatened with extinction. Apart from the Pyramids, which according to legend were built against a catastrophe to hold the wisdom the human race had gained, there may have been many other such secret storehouses scattered around the world. Perhaps underneath the great artificial hill of Silbury in England there were such chambers, and the recently discovered underground chambers in South America and Turkey may also have held archives of scientific knowledge.

Also it appears that some fragments of knowledge from a high culture survived in oral traditions, as witness the legend of Sirius' dark companion from the Dogons of the Sudan. By a quirk of fate, it appears that this fragment was remembered by someone and the story was handed down the ages, while almost everything else was forgotten. We have also suggested that the scientific knowledge of the ancient Greeks was gained from the great libraries in Egypt, and that this knowledge stemmed originally from what was saved from within the pyramids. There were a great many libraries in the ancient world, and little except scattered fragments of their literature has survived to the present day.

Apart from the libraries of Alexandria and the Temple of Ptah, there have been many 'burnings of the books' in antiquity. The library of Pergamus in Asia Minor contained 200,000 books. This too was destroyed.

When the Romans destroyed Carthage in the Punic Wars

in 146 BC, they burned to ashes the library said to contain half a million volumes. The Romans also destroyed, under the leadership of Julius Caesar, the Druidic library at Autun in France, containing thousands of scrolls on philosophy, medicine, astronomy and mathematics.

In China, the Emperor Tsin Shin Hwang-ti ordered all the ancient books destroyed in 213 BC.

Leo Isaurus burned 300,000 books in Byzantium in the eighth century AD. The Catholic Church's Inquisition in the Middle Ages destroyed vast and unknown numbers of heretical works of literature, which, because of their pagan origins, were anti-Christian and therefore works of the Devil.

It is probably true that Medieval Christianity was responsible for the loss of irreplaceable knowledge and held the human mind in the bondage of a mental Dark Age for centuries. Not only did Christians eliminate great areas of forbidden knowledge in Europe, but in their voyages to the New World they destroyed the literature of ancient cultures far superior in many ways to that of the Europeans of the time, and in the process eliminated two great civilisations, that of the Aztec and the Inca.

In Yucatan, a young Catholic Spanish monk, Diego de Landa, discovered a large library of Maya manuscripts. 'We burned them all because they contained nothing except superstition and the machinations of the Devil,' he said. To this day, the surviving inscriptions of Maya glyphs have never been deciphered, except for some mathematical symbols, and those without any degree of absolute certainty. Considering the extent of the fragmentary knowledge contained in the almost only surviving work, the Popol Vuh, the 'Bible' of the Central American peoples, it is possible that the loss of knowledge suffered was almost as great as that caused by the destruction of books in the Mediterranean world.

Not all the blame, however, can be laid at the hands of the Asians and Europeans. When the Spaniards entered Peru, they found a civilisation highly advanced, well organised and with a strong central government more efficient than any possessed by the Europeans of the time. They found well maintained public works; roads and bridges well maintained, irrigation, water supply and public buildings, food production and storage, and supplies of all kinds carefully controlled in a balanced and efficient economy. It was a huge, well-knit empire, which functioned perfectly under the Royal Inca, yet without any written language or mnemonic devices except the records maintained by a system of quipos, or knotted strings, and without the use of a monetary system. The Inca had a superstitious fear of writing. The official explanation given to the Spaniards was that at a time of great epidemic the oracle said that writing had to be done away with under the penalty of death. It appears then that writing had been known in the earliest phases of Inca rule, and was eliminated. This seems to parallel the Chinese destruction of books in 213 BC, when all the knowledge was eliminated. Was it really writing the Incas were afraid of, or what the writings may have contained? If they were aware of the nature of the conflict which had destroyed a civilisation and almost mankind itself, then perhaps they considered that the written knowledge posed a menace to future ages, and destroyed it. Perhaps the long-vanished writings of the Incas held the same sort of knowledge as many Sanskrit texts which refer to nuclear weapons. If this knowledge was possibly considered far too dangerous to survive, who can blame them? Even in our day, many of the scientists concerned with the making of the first nuclear bomb would have preferred this knowledge to have remained only in the realm of theory. At best, they hoped the device would not work in practice.

Was this Inca legend of a pestilence connected with atomic weapons and their effects? There are fused areas in South America, and also in North America from where the ancestors of the Incas may have fled, which remind us strongly of the vitrified areas created by modern nuclear tests.

If we assumed that the Incas never possessed, knew of or invented a written language, then we would be unable to explain the existence of a written language which has been discovered in South America. As we have seen, thousands of leaf-thin gold plates were discovered in deep underground caverns in Ecuador, and the language appears to have been neither glyphic nor pictorial, but *alphabetical*. Furthermore, this alphabetical writing bears a resemblance to ancient Cretan and Sanskrit scripts – was this the type of writing which was eliminated from human memory by the Incas?

In this connection, it is of interest to observe that the Maya have a legend about their 'Golden Book', a history of the Maya written on leaf-thin gold plates, and which were hidden at the time of the Conquest to prevent them falling into the hands of the Spaniards. These plates have never been found, so the existence of such plates in Ecuador should encourage the belief that the Maya were dealing in realities when they spoke of the Golden Book, which has never been found to this day. The fact that similar things have been found means that the Maya Golden Book could exist and there are Maya legends about secret underground places which were built long ago. Perhaps one day further discoveries of this nature will come to light, though unless we find the key to decipher this unknown language, we may still learn nothing from them.

It may seem that there has been both a deliberate and sub-conscious urge throughout history to eliminate ancient recorded knowledge. That which was not destroyed, either accidentally or by design in wars, was deliberately suppressed because it was *dangerous*. Possibly, some of these attempts were well-meaning; it has not mattered in the final analysis – we have found our own road to possible hell.

Unfortunately, however, the destruction of knowledge was not selective; the good was destroyed along with the bad. Most areas of knowledge, whether it be nuclear physics, the secret of flight, knowledge of explosives, biology and medicine, have applications which are both good and bad. Perhaps it was considered that the dangers of the bad outweighed the advantages of the good.

The fact that ancient knowledge existed in many fields shows that the knowledge that existed in, for example, astronomy was not an isolated freak, but the inheritance of an advanced and balanced culture, which is paralleled by present-day civilisation.

There exists a great storehouse of ancient knowledge in the field of biology: many of the cures claimed by the people known as witches would seem to be handed down from a very distant tradition, as may be many medical remedies handed on by ancient rural practices. It is now known that the old folk cure of sepsis – that of using the mould of a potato or fruit – is actually a primitive version of penicillin. It seems that even in very early times the curative properties of moulds was known, because in Ancient Egypt a papyrus of the eleventh Dynasty tells of a fungus grown on still water which possessed curative properties for wounds and open sores.[1] Warmed soil and soya-bean curd, both of which have anti-biotic properties, were used in Ancient China and Greece.

Skulls unearthed from Dynastic Egypt have been found to contain artificial teeth, and crowns and fillings have been observed in teeth from skulls in Campeche, Mexico, which date from the Maya civilisation.

Although most of modern medical and surgical practices are based on knowledge which has come down to us from ancient Egypt, Bablylon and Greece, the medical and surgical abilities of the Peruvian coastal cultures were as great, if not greater than, those possessed by the Mediterranean peoples. Possibly the reason this fact has largely been overlooked or ignored is that these civilisations flourished in isolation from the rest of the world until the sixteenth century, and no written treatise on their medical skills has been made or passed on to us. In pre-Columbian Peru, we have no medical heroes such as Hippocrates to inspire Western medical techniques.

However, the discovery of a great many pottery vessels from the coastal Chimu culture has revealed remarkable life-like portrayals of every aspect of Chimu life, including many on medical skills. It appears that these ancient people performed many delicate operations: they amputated limbs, and fitted artificial legs, arms and even hands. When one considers the excellence of wood carving from the Peruvian coastal region, it is not too surprising that they were able to make accurate models of human limbs, but what is surprising is that they were able to carry out major amputation operations with such good results that the patients were able to recover to use artificial limbs to replace those they had lost.

1. See H. M. Botcher, *Miracle Drugs*, Heinemann, London, 1963.

Even in nineteenth-century Europe, major amputation invariably resulted in death from shock, due to the crude methods and lack of anaesthetics, or from sepsis caused by the total lack of hygiene.

Some form of anaesthetic must have been known to the Chimu surgeons. Some pottery vessels show internal operations being performed, including abdominal operations, which could scarcely have been carried out without anaesthetics of some kind. In China, acupuncture has been carried out for an unknown period of time, and is apparently effective even for major operations, both on human beings and animals. Is it possible that this may have been used by the South American peoples? It has been suggested in recent years that contact between ancient China and the American pre-Columbian civilisations was not unknown. It is thought that some of the Mayan art forms, and the traditions of many American Indian tribes, particularly those from New Mexico, show an affinity with Chinese art and traditions; and it has also been suggested that some of the Mexican glyphs which have been found at Monte Alban and Teotehuacan show an affinity with archaic Chinese. Contacts between these peoples in art and tradition would also mean an exchange of trade – and knowledge. It is thus possible that acupuncture as a medical aid was not limited to ancient China.

Old Sanskrit texts reveal that ancient India had an extensive knowledge of medicine, including the circulatory and nervous systems. Indian doctors performed Caesarian operations, trephined for brain surgery and used anaesthetics. Sushruta in the fifth century BC listed the diagnosis of 1120 diseases and described 121 surgical instruments.

A Brahmin book, the Sactya Grantham, described vaccination in 1500 BC, centuries before the credit was given to Edward Jenner (1749–1833), as follows:

'Take on the tip of a knife the contents of the inflammation, inject it into the arm of a man, mixing it with his blood. A fever will follow but the malady will pass very easily and create no complications.'

A magic mirror which could illuminate the bones of the body was said to be possessed by the Chinese Emperor Tsin-

Shi (259–210 BC) and was kept in the palace of Hien-Yang in 206 BC. The instrument was used for medical purposes. X-rays in antiquity? Here one is reminded of a drawing found in Mexico, which shows a human figure with a rectangle over the chest area and within the area of the rectangle there appears a stylised drawing of what appears to be the spinal column and ribs. The significance of this drawing has escaped the anthropologists and archaeologists, and the only logical explanation is that it is a drawing of an X-ray device in operation. Here again, has this a connection with Chinese visits to the Americas, or is it once again a demonstration of advanced medical techniques in ancient America? For the surgical techniques we have observed among the Chimu, some sort of X-ray device as an aid to diagnosis would be virtually a necessity. It has been assumed that the Chimu, as other American pre-Columbian cultures, had no knowledge of electricity. This would be essential if some sort of fluoroscopes were used. But it is interesting to observe that the Chimu plated objects with gold in a way which today can only be done by electrolysis. We remember that ancient batteries were discovered in the Middle East, and it is not impossible that a form of electricity was also known in the New World.

The Aborigines of Australia have practised blood transfusions for many thousands of years, and their women have oral contraceptives made from the resin of a particular plant. Apparently, unlike our artificially developed oral contraceptives, these have no harmful side-effects, and are chiefly used in periods of drought or food shortages, so that children are not born who cannot be fed. It is a sensible method of population control which many countries in South-east Asia particularly could copy. The Aborigines pose something of a riddle to anthropologists, as they appear to be a remnant of a highly advanced people forced to live exceedingly primitive lives in a hostile environment. Possibly, these medical skills are but two things which have been remembered and passed down through tribal lore from a remote period, whilst almost everything else has been forgotten. The Aborigines also possess a most useful weapon and tool for food hunting in the shape of the boomerang, which has been described as a very efficient aerodynamic shape which could scarcely have been invented by pure primitives in a random fashion. Here again, this may be an echo from an earlier epoch, when a weapon was invented, drawing upon scientific skills, for use by people deprived of all but the most basic implements for survival. There is no measure of agreement among anthropologists regarding the origin of the Aborigine, and although it is generally agreed that he was not originally indigenous to Australia, but arrived from elsewhere, estimates vary as to the time of his arrival from 20,000 years to 10,000 years ago. His racial stock is uncertain, but he has been described as an archaic Caucasoid, due to his heavy facial and body-hair absent in both Mongol and Negroids; and his dark colouring is assumed to be an adaptation to hot desert conditions. The Aborigine has a level of intelligence which is not less than that of any other peoples on Earth, and he would indeed need a high level of intelligence to adapt successfully to the hostile environment in which he has lived.

Another aspect of biological techniques is concerned with plant and animal husbandry. We have never with any certainty been able to identify the wild ancestors of maize-corn or even wheat. The wild ancestor of maize has never been traced, but is known to have existed in a cultivated form in South America for more than 4,000 years. Although unknown in the Old World at one time, maize is now grown in many parts of the world, and forms part of the staple diet of many peoples far removed from the area of its original cultivation. Wheat is generally supposed to have been developed from a wild ancestor called emma and was first cultivated in the Middle East region as long ago as 8,000 years. Perhaps this is not really so; what we call the wild ancestral form could be a degenerate species of a once-cultivated form which had grown wild and unattended for thousands of years?

In South America the Inca were great agriculturalists, and had developed many food plants some of the varieties of which, since died out due to the destruction of the Inca empire and the subsequent collapse of its agricultural system, we today have been unable to duplicate. The Inca grew maize, gourds and squashes, a great variety of beans, and many varieties of potatoes, one of which, a frost-resistant variety grown high in the Andes, has now vanished and the secret of its cultivation with it.

The Maya today make soap from a tree which is called, appropriately, the soapberry tree, and they also produce honey from *stingless* bees. There is an old Maya legend that Quetzelcoatl, the culture god of Central America, developed cotton plants which grew different-coloured cottons. Cotton today grows in only one colour – white – and the other colours have to be produced by dyeing, but before we dismiss this idea of different coloured cottons as impossible, we have to remember the different coloured flowers which we have produced by selective breeding in recent times. Perhaps something akin to this was also done in the past. The cultivation of different colours in cotton would be extremely useful and save a great deal of time and effort in the dyeing of fabrics.

The popular flower the Dahlia was brought to Europe by the Conquistadores from Mexico where it was grown by the Aztecs in great profusion and variety, yet no wild ancestor of the tuber has ever been located. If we cannot trace wild ancestors for many of our most useful and ornamental plants, when could they ever be said to have been wild? And if they were never wild, where did they come from in the first place? Were they imported, originally, along with the colonists, from another world where they were developed by biological engineering, for use in a new planetary environment? Many of our cultivated species, if left to their own devices, would rapidly be overwhelmed by wild vegetation and would die out. Wheat has to be cultivated artificially, otherwise it will degenerate and be vanquished by wild grasses. Could these, at a remote time, have been highly-cultivated plants which degenerated when the planet reverted to a wilderness state? We have seen this happen in the case of the Inca empire, where plants have vanished due to lack of cultivation.

We have developed many useful plants from wild ancestors, it is true, by selective breeding and careful cultivation. This brings us to another point, which creates a puzzle. We have seen that the master blueprint for all forms of life is contained within the DNA structure which determines all the possible characteristics of each particular form. Therefore, all the variations inherent in any particular species are already coded in the DNA, and selective breeding (which is how plants are improved) is done by selecting certain characteristics which are *already there*. We cannot create a new plant for which the potential does not exist in the DNA, which is possibly why we have been unable to produce a true black rose or daffodil. If the potential for this characteristic does not exist within the DNA molecule of the particular plant, then we shall forever be unable to produce it. Therefore, no matter how many variations we produce from a 'wild' ancestor in a cultivated state, we are only selectively using capabilities which already exist, but are not utilised, because they are not necessary for survival in a wild state, or they even detract from useful survival characteristics. Bearing these facts in mind, can we not see cultivated plants as descendants not of wild plants, but of plants once domesticated and which reverted to the wild state, their specialised characteristics becoming dormant over the ages the better to enable them to survive in a wild environment? This idea again connects with the ancient concept of a 'Garden Paradise' which later reverted to the wild. The development of plant cultivation such as that of the Peruvian region both among the Inca and pre-Inca peoples presupposes a long period of development, *or* the inheritance of a great fund of knowledge in plant husbandry and genetics.

It may appear that some knowledge has been inherited from a scientific past where a great deal was known of the properties of different plants; otherwise how were special products known to the ancients, or to present-day primitive peoples?

Not only do the Australian Aborigines use a plant-derived oral contraceptive, but the forest natives of New Guinea use the same technique. Amazon Indians pulp the leaves of a certain plant to use as a very efficient antibiotic against jungle ulcers which even penicillin will not wholly cure. Did they evolve these methods by trial and error over a long period of time, and if so, what idea led them to experiment in this manner? It may seem that by trial and error alone they could never have stumbled across the properties of many of these plants. Or were their scientific ancestors aware of these properties by the use of analytical methods before they were thrust into a savage and primitive environment? Was it inherited by oral tradition in the same way that the Dogon of the Sudan have certain scraps of knowledge of the stars?

It has often been said that the great divergence between cultivated plants in the Old World and in the New points to a completely separate development of civilisation in each hemisphere. It is said that if there had been transoceanic contacts between the civilisation of the Old World and those of the Americas, many plants would have been diffused on both sides of the Atlantic, and that maize, for example, would have been grown in Asia and Africa thousands of years ago as well as in America. The peoples would have carried seeds and plants with them by way of trade. This is, of course, supposing that the world was in a fairly primitive state. However, if we assume that there had existed a world civilisation comparable to our own of which little trace remains today, then this factor of separate growth areas may not be as significant. For example, today, an almost staple drink in England is tea, vast quantities of which are used each year – but tea, the tea plant itself, is not, and cannot grow in the temperate climate of England, except under artificial and experimental conditions which are therefore not commercially viable.

A future plant biologist, therefore, living thousands of years after our civilisation has ceased to exist, may never suspect that the English drank tea, because the plant for its production *did not grow in that region.*

In the same way, an advanced civilisation of the past may have selected certain areas where certain plants were best adapted, and cultivated them intensively for distribution *around the world.* Being extremely perishable consumer goods, it is almost certain they would leave no traces in the country of their importation, especially after a great period of time.

The great differences in disease rates among pre-Columbian civilisations and those of the Old World has been cited as another reason for separate development. Many European diseases were completely unknown to both the American Indians and Polynesians until they made contact with Europeans, and with their lack of resistance, whole populations were decimated. However, if all diseases had developed naturally, and micro-organisms were part of the planetary ecology, there should, in nature, be no reason why one continental mass should suffer and the other escape. If disease, however, was loosed artificially – we have previously mentioned the possibility of bacteriological warfare – then it is possible either that this form of warfare was geographically limited, or that some populations were able to prepare forms of defence against it. Admittedly, answers of this kind to the separate development theory are tentative, but they are possibilities, particularly if we assume that a highly developed civilisation existed in the remote past.

Turning now to the fields of more mechanical inventiveness, we find mention in ancient records of many things commonplace in our twentieth century. Descriptions by ancient writers and references in mythologies lead us to suppose that some form of artificial lighting, perhaps electric, existed, as well as extremely accurate map-making (which requires advanced surveying techniques and instrumentation), robots, microscopes and telescopes. We have already mentioned the evidence for astronomical knowledge, as well as the possibilities that radio, radar and aircraft had been developed.

Electricity is supposed to be a recent invention, but we have already seen that for the ancients to have possessed X-ray equipment they must also have had a form of electricity, and the possession of this form of power would explain the gold-plating which cannot be explained any other way.

The German archaeologist Wilhelm Konig found near Baghdad in 1938–9 a number of earthenware jars with necks covered with asphalt and iron rods encased within copper cylinders. He thought they were ancient electric batteries.

Willard Grey of GEC after World War II made duplicates of these ancient batteries, using copper sulphate instead of the unknown electrolyte which had dissipated, and the battery worked. This seemed to point to the fact that the Ancient Babylonians knew of electricity. Electro-plated articles have been unearthed in the same general area which supports this view.

Prof Dennis Saurat has found remains that he considers to be those of electrical devices in Ancient Egypt. The rock tombs of Abu Simbel have always posed a great puzzle, as it is known that the interior chambers which were cut from the solid rock were painted in great detail after they were made – yet no trace of fire blackening has been found, as would be the case if ordinary torches had been used. No trace of fire blackening from antiquity has been found in any Egyptian building where artificial illumination would be needed. Did, then, the ancient Egyptians use electric torches, perhaps carefully preserved from an earlier age?

Ever-burning lamps are frequently mentioned in historical documents.

Numa Pompilius, king of Rome, had a perpetual lamp shining in the dome of a temple. Plutarch mentioned a lamp which burned at the entrance to a temple of Jupiter-Ammon, whose priests claimed it had burned for centuries.

Pausanius described a golden lamp which could burn for a year in the Temple of Minerva. St Augustine (AD 354–430) told of a temple dedicated to Isis where there was a lamp that neither wind nor water could extinguish. This description is remarkably like that of an electric lamp which cannot be affected by wind or water, unlike an ordinary flame torch. An inscription indicated that a lamp burning at Antioch during the reign of Justinian (sixth century AD) had burned for five centuries.

In the Middle Ages a perpetual lamp was found in England that had been functioning for several centuries.

There is an old Sanskrit text called the Agastya Samhita which gave instructions for making batteries:

Place a well-cleaned copper plate in an earthenware vessel. Cover it first with copper sulphate and then with moist sawdust. After that put a mercury-amalgamated zinc sheet on top of the sawdust to avoid polarization.

The contact will produce an energy known by the twin name of Mitra-Varuna. Water will be split into Prana-vayu and Udanavayu. A chain of one hundred jars is said to give a very active and effective force.

Mitra-Varuna is now cathode-anode. Pranavayu and Udanavayu are oxygen and hydrogen respectively.

Electricity in Europe, the Middle and Far East in an ancient era. Fables? The same stories are reflected on the other side of the world in the Americas.

The Maya have stories of the cities which were lit by day and night. Many ancient Maya buildings have no windows, and yet there also, like in the ancient Egyptian structures, there is no trace of fire blackening inside these dark, painted chambers. Even the Amazon Indians have legends of the cities of ancient times which were lit by 'stars' – electric lights? These stories were told the Spaniards hundreds of years ago, so this is not something which has filtered down to these jungle tribes from recent times.

Gold objects have been found which have been plated in a manner which today can only be matched by electrolysis, notably in the area of the old Chimu capital, Chan-Chan. Also in the Americas, there have been discovered objects made of platinum (which the Spaniards discarded as useless) which requires temperatures of 9,000°C for smelting, and temperatures of this range cannot be produced by ordinary fires.

In Greek legend, Hephaestos, the blacksmith of the Olympian gods, had two golden maidens for servants. 'They are made of metal,' he explained, 'but they do my bidding, and have thoughts in their heads.' Robots? It will be remembered that it was Hephaestos who built Talos, the metal giant who guarded Crete and who threatened anyone who landed. Was this also a robot, programmed to do certain actions and carry out certain tasks? When Jason attacked the heel of Talos, was he perhaps switching its power supply off, or disconnecting it in some manner? If these robots had been built by one of the Greek gods, then they must be presumed to stem from a remoter era than that of Greek civilisation. Powered perhaps by solar cells, and functioning for centuries? Once they broke down they would be broken up and melted to be turned into spear and javelin heads.

In China also there are reports of mechanical men in antiquity. The Emperor Ta-chouan possessed one, and the jealous emperor had it broken up because the empress coveted it.

We have the curious phenomenon in ancient times of the oracles, who could deliver wisdom. There was the Oracle of Delphi in Greece, and there were temples in Egypt where the statues could speak. No doubt some of it was trickery, operated by hidden priests, but is it also not possible that some of these things may refer to ancient computers which were still functioning centuries after their makers became dust?

Garsilaso de la Vega was told that the Incas had a statue in the valley of Rimac 'which spoke and gave answers to questions like the Delphic Apollo'. Could this perhaps have been a form of computer?

If an ancient highly advanced culture had collapsed, among the measures taken to preserve a degree of civilisation may have been the installation of computers programmed with information useful to the survivors struggling back to civilisation. It is not unlikely that we ourselves, should our civilisation be menaced with almost total destruction in, say, a nuclear war, would prepare and programme computers with information for those survivors who asked for it.

Sponge divers near the island of Antikythera in 1900 found a metallic object which, when it was cleaned, was found to consist of a system of complex cogs and gears. Dr Derek J. de Solla Price, a scientist working at the Institute for Advanced Studies at Princeton, USA, who examined the object, said:

It appears that this was, indeed, a computing machine that could work out and exhibit the motions of the Sun and Moon and probably also the planets.

The date ascribed to this device was approximately 65 BC, and came as a surprise to modern scientists who had never suspected that the Greeks had anything like this – nothing like it had been discovered before among Grecian artifacts.

It is said that such a device must have had a long history of development behind it. 'Finding a thing like this is like finding a jet plane in the tomb of Tutankhamun,' said Dr Price at a meeting in Washington in 1959.

The source of the discovery of this calculating machine is interesting, as it was found in the sea among amphorae, which may lead us to suspect it was possibly being carried in a ship which was wrecked. We can ask ourselves: if this was being carried in a ship, was it being taken somewhere *from* Greece, or was it being *brought to Greece* from somewhere? Nothing like this had been found in Greece before, and it may be pertinent to note that it was to measure the movements of the Sun and the Moon, primarily, that the instrument was designed. We are not yet certain that it calculated the movement of the planets. We suggested in *Colony: Earth* that Stonehenge was a computer built for a specific purpose, and that was to study the movement relating to the *Earth, Moon and Sun only*, that it was not built by the Greeks (as has often been thought) but that the Greeks went to Stonehenge to study these motions and learn from the Stonehenge mathematicians. Was the computer, then, either built in Britain, or based on data obtained from the Stonehenge computer?

This would mean that Egypt was not the only place where the Greek students went to gather their knowledge, but that much of their mathematical expertise was in fact learned from the mathematicians who lived in the far north land of the Hyperboreans, where there was a round temple of astronomy and mathematics. The fact that the Greeks frequently alluded to this northern land points to Britain and Stonehenge.

9

Horizons of Yesterday

In late Medieval times in Europe, the world was a curiously shrunken place. The region of Europe and the Mediterranean was known, although not to the mass of the people, and there was a vague knowledge that there was a country called India and another called Cathay (China), and even that there were some islands off the coast of China. There were no maps being drawn up which were by any means accurate. Europeans were unaware, at that time, of the islands of the Pacific, or the continent of Australia, the islands of New Zealand, or the southern part of Africa. They knew a little of China from the tales brought back by Marco Polo; of the Americas and the teeming advanced civilisations and the great stone cities that existed there they were totally ignorant until the opening of the New World in the late fifteenth and early sixteenth centuries by the Spaniards.

Most Europeans of the time thought that the Earth was flat and that to sail too far across the Atlantic Ocean was to face certain death by falling over the edge. Some thought that far out at sea was a belt of fire girdling the earth, which also meant certain death. So until Columbus and Vespucci sailed in their little ships, the explorations of the Europeans were severely limited.

Further back, in late Roman times, humanity fared little better. Civilised men of the time viewed the whole world as encompassed by the Mediterranean and the lands surrounding it, although India was known – the Western coast – to the Romans. Britain was known, of course, and there was a suspicion that there were colder lands further north where the sea rovers lived, but none went there. There were even more vague stories of islands which lay over the great ocean, but there were neither the ships nor the men to venture so far away.

Yet, surprisingly, the further we go back in time, the *wider* these shrunken horizons become, which surely is the opposite to what should be the case?

The Ancient Egyptians circumnavigated Africa, although this was forgotten by the time the Romans had conquered Egypt.

The Ancient Greeks apparently either knew or suspected that other great lands existed apart from the known Mediterranean world. Once again, can we not think that this also was knowledge gained from their studies in the archives of Egypt?

Philostratus of Athens (AD 175–249) said: 'If the land be considered in relation to the entire mass of water, we can show that the earth is the lesser of the two.' This alone points to a knowledge of the comparative masses of land and sea, which could possibly have been gained by a study of ancient maps.

Plato said in Phaedo that the people of the Mediterranean occupied only a small portion of the Earth.

Pytheas of Marseilles (330 BC) voyaged to the Arctic Circle and described the Midnight Sun.

Seneca may have heard of the Americas, because a verse in Medea says:

> There shall come a time
> When the bands of Ocean
> Shall be loosened
> And the vast Earth shall be laid open
> Another Tiphys shall disclose new worlds
> And lands shall be seen beyond Thule.

Thule was the ancient name for Iceland, and new lands beyond must obviously refer to North America.

The Vishnu Purana, a Sanskrit text, describes a Pushkar (continent) with two Varshas (lands) at the foot of Meru (North Pole), and this continent faces Kshira (an ocean of milk) and the two lands are shaped like a bow. What sounds like a mythical fairy tale is in reality a close description of the Americas. The two lands (North and South America) face the Arctic Ocean (the Ocean of Milk – presumably because of the ice), they lie under the North Pole, and their shape could be described as a bow.

As so much else in ancient texts from India, this again seems to be knowledge which has been passed down from a very remote period, as the Hindus of 2,000 years ago did not have sea-going vessels capable of making the voyage to the Americas. No doubt the Brahmin priests of 2,000 years ago did not themselves understand the meaning of this description, but as with the mathematical texts they merely copied faithfully the sacred writings.

The Bon sect of Tibet possess an ancient book which contains a chart marked off into squares and rectangles with the names of unknown countries. The Soviet philologist Bronislav Kouznetsov came to the conclusion that the chart was a map, and identified the Persian city of Pasargady (fourth to seventh century BC), Alexandria, Jerusalem, the countries of Bactria, Babylonia, North Persia and the Caspian Sea. The remote Tibetans, locked within their high mountain fastness, then, had a great deal of geographical knowledge many centuries ago.

The most extraordinary discoveries made in recent years, however, have been the maps of Admiral Piri Reis, two of which, dated 1513 and 1528, have been verified as genuine both by the American Geographical Society and the Royal Geographical Society of Great Britain.

The map dated 1513 shows Brittany, Spain, West Africa, the Atlantic, part of North America and a complete outline of the eastern half of South America. At the bottom of the map is shown the coastline of Antarctica, eastward to a point under Africa.

The second map – that dated 1528 – shows Greenland, Labrador, part of Canada and the east coast of North America down to Florida.

It is suspected that these two maps are but a part of a world mapping series, perhaps also showing the Indian Ocean and the entire Pacific region, although these have never been discovered.

There is another map, belonging to Orontus Finaeus, dated 1531, which also shows the outline of the Antarctic Continent. This shows rivers and mountain ranges.

In Iceland was discovered the map of Zeno, which shows Greenland as three islands under the ice cap, and rivers and mountains clearly marked. This map is dated even earlier than the maps of the Americas and Antarctica, in fact 1380.

There are many peculiarities about these maps, which in themselves indicate a totally different knowledge of the world in antiquity to that suspected until now, and also indicates a very different world to the one we live in at the present time.

First let us deal with the Piri Reis maps. The Turkish Admiral Piri Reis compiled an atlas called the Book of the Seas containing two hundred and ten well-drawn maps, and the origin of the two Antarctic maps is amazing. According to notes made by Piri Reis, his uncle Captain Kemel captured a Spanish sailor during the course of a naval battle. This sailor had in his possession some rare maps, which he claimed were the ones used by Columbus in his discovery of the New World. This sailor had in fact been on three of Columbus' expeditions. The sailor said, under questioning:
'A certain book from the time of Alexander the Great was translated in Europe, and after reading it Christopher Columbus went and discovered the Antilles with the vessels he obtained from the Spanish government.'

It appears, therefore, that Columbus did not sail blindly across the Atlantic Ocean in his quest for the New World, but that he had in fact in his possession extremely accurate maps so that he knew exactly where he was going. This is further borne out by the story that Columbus described the shape of the world as slightly pear-shaped. As we have only recently discovered this fact ourselves from our voyages in space, he must have obtained the information from a very ancient source.

The problem is this: at the time of Alexander the Great, these maps could not have been originals, because the knowledge of the Greeks of that time was insufficient for them to have drawn them. They neither travelled such distances nor had the necessary surveying equipment to draw the maps. We can only conclude that at the time of Alexander the Great the maps were copies of charts even more remotely ancient. Once again, does it not seem possible that this is further knowledge which some unknown Greek student had gleaned from the libraries of Alexandria, which were said to contain all the knowledge of the human race from a remote time?

Examination of the maps has shown them to be incredibly accurate. The American cartographer Arlington H. Mallery, with the co-operation of the US Navy Hydrographic Office, determined that the distances between Europe, Africa and the Americas on the Piri Reis maps were exact. Until the eighteenth century no longitudes had been determined with any accuracy.

The chart of South America shows the rivers Orinoco, Amazon, Parana, Uruguay and Rio de la Plata with extreme accuracy, yet none of the explorers of the southern Atlantic at this time – Vespucci, Magellan or Columbus – had charted the rivers of South America beyond the coastal deltas. Therefore, the continents of North and South America were mapped with extreme accuracy not only before the time of the fifteenth-century explorers, *but before the time of Alexander the Great.*

It is when we look at the portions dealing with Antarctica that we confront the greatest mysteries, however. Both the Piri Reis maps and that of Orontus Finaeus accurately chart the outline of the continent, and show rivers and mountain ranges. For one thing, in historic times, the first explorations of Antarctica did not begin until the nineteenth century, and no really accurate mapping was completed until the International Geophysical Year 1951. When the survey was completed the old map was compared with the seismic soundings taken in 1951. A discrepancy was discovered and a second seismic probe undertaken. It was then discovered that an error had been made – the ancient Piri Reis map was not in error, as had been thought. The old map was more accurate than the modern ones.

The other peculiarity about the Antarctic maps is that they show mountain ranges and river courses whose existence was not formerly suspected, and not charted until the I.G.Y. of 1951. The fact that the ancient maps show the continent as it is *without the ice* leads to the conclusion, unwelcome though it may be to many scientists, that the maps were drawn at a time when there was *no ice at the South Pole*.

The map of Zeno, showing Greenland, was likewise checked by the French Polar Expedition of Paul-Emile Victor in 1947–9. Again, the ancient map was found to be extraordinarily accurate, and, like the maps of Antarctica, had apparently been drawn up when the North Polar regions were ice-free.

This must surely be a hard pill for the scientists to swallow. It does not matter which view point is taken, these maps are totally opposed to all traditional scientific thinking regarding the Earth's climatic history. Most scientists have been of the opinion – and still are – that the two Polar regions have been sealed under the ice for many hundreds of thousands of years, being either larger or smaller depending on the fluctuation of the glaciations. On the one hand, they must take the view that the maps were drawn up hundreds of thousands or even over a million years ago – according to the anthropologists – before the human race appeared on the planet. If we admit that human beings intelligent enough and of a high enough level of civilisation to draw up such accurate maps existed so long ago, then all the scientists' carefully worked out evolutionary models are complete nonsense. If, on the other hand, the scientists conclude that they could not possibly have been drawn up at such a remote date, but between six to eight thousand years ago, then their hypothesis of an Ice Age and the Polar Ice Caps being in existence at this time are false. Cores taken from the sediments of the Ross Sea in Antarctica indicate that vegetation of a subtropical nature was growing at the South Pole some 6,000 years ago, and the presence of fossils of orange and magnolia trees in the North Polar regions also indicate a much warmer climate with *no glaciation* in this area only a few thousand years ago.

These maps alone should cause a revolution in considering the past, and they point to two factors in particular which have never been taken into account by our scientists. One is that our ideas regarding the Earth's climate 6,000 to 8,000 years ago are in error, and that quite possibly the idea of an Ice Age in the past is totally erroneous – as was pointed out in *Colony: Earth*. The second factor is that as the ancient Greeks at the time of Alexander the Great were incapable of drawing up such accurate charts, and certainly no one later than this was capable either, they must have been drawn up at an earlier date, which means that a level of culture existed which has disappeared. This idea also is completely at variance with all the hypotheses at present in vogue among the cultural anthropologists regarding man's state of advancement during the past 10,000 or 12,000 years.

Arlington Mallery says: 'We don't know how they could map it so accurately without an aeroplane.'

We have already mentioned aircraft at a prehistoric period about which little is known apart from legends, and it appears that these maps must stem from this period. From such accurate maps – even more accurate than modern ones – a lot can be inferred. The people who undertook this mapping must have been in possession of advanced surveying equipment – for us to map as accurately we have to resort to photography from aircraft, so we can assume that the ancient mapmakers probably did likewise. Also, the surveyors either travelled to Antarctica from bases elsewhere, in which case they needed long-distance aircraft or powerful ocean-going ships; or, if it is true that Antarctica was free of ice at this time, they could have operated from bases within the present Antarctic continent itself, which would lead us to suspect that Antarctica was inhabited at this point in time. It is perhaps significant to note that Piri Reis said that the atlas contained charts of all *inhabited* lands, which must therefore include the present South Polar regions. It is the opinion of the author that many surprises await us in the Antarctic continent, and it is more than likely that if we ever are able to excavate the land which now lies under thousands of feet of ice we may discover not only traces of human habitation from the legendary past, but the ruins of cities whose existence has never been suspected. Perhaps Antarctica was one of the main continents where the ancient civilisation of marvels described in the ancient legends reached its full flowering.

Our inference of the techniques possessed by the ancient surveyors leads us to the conclusion that they used advanced surveying instruments, photography and also possibly air-craft. These things also indicate a complex, organised and highly advanced technology on at least a level with our own, as such devices would not develop in isolation, but only as part of a highly developed civilisation.

It is beginning to appear that long ago the whole planet was as accurately mapped as it is today, since we have in our possession detailed charts of the entire western half of the globe. Although no maps of comparable accuracy exist of the Asian continents, it is surely not mere fantasy to suspect that they must also have existed, although they have not been found. There is always the possibility that they will be discovered one day. On the other hand, the existing maps may have survived the ravages of time only by a fluke of fate, and the others may have disappeared for ever.

Even so, the existence of these maps is further evidence for something which was suggested earlier in this book. If the whole world was accurately mapped, does this fact not point to the existence of a *world-wide civilisation*? As we mentioned earlier, only such a civilisation can account for the widespread legend of a Golden Age, and this is why re-searchers seek in vain for an isolated location for the original 'Atlantis' or mother-culture.

It may well be that if our civilisation is destroyed in a nuclear disaster, sages in future times will in their turn seek in vain for their Atlantis, being ignorant of the fact that the twentieth-century technological culture had spread all over the planet.

It is not the fault of the Mediterranean peoples or those of Northern Europe that their horizons shrank so drastically over the past 4,000 years or so. The civilisations of the Americas were likewise in their isolation unaware of peoples across the other side of the great ocean barriers. They pos-sessed legends of white teachers who came from far across the sea, but they did not appear to wonder from what distant lands they may have come, or make any attempt to under-take voyages to discover these distant lands. Of course, the Peruvian peoples such as the Chimu and the Inca lived on the Pacific coast, and the Toltec and Aztec lived far inland in Mexico, but even that other advanced race of the Americas, the Maya, many of whose towns were built on the coast facing the Atlantic, never attempted ocean voyages. Of all the peoples of the Americas, it was the Maya who may have sailed eastwards; but they never produced an American Columbus to discover a New World in Europe or Africa.

We can now postulate that at a period we term pre-historic there existed a civilisation whose members were aware of the shape of the earth and the distribution of the masses of land and sea. No doubt they were aware of all the lands that existed and all the major foci of population, in the same way that the average educated man today has at least a general knowledge of continental lands and distances, and the distribution of the world's major cities. The fact that this knowledge was almost completely forgotten can be best explained by a catastrophe which wiped out civilisation on a *planetary scale*.

It can be demonstrated how easily civilisation can be completely disrupted by taking as an example the destruction of the Roman Empire. With the collapse of Roman order in the fifth century AD, outlying provinces such as Britain quickly lapsed into a state of barbarism. Within several centuries the Roman presence was almost forgotten, so much so that by the time of the Norman conquest the remains of the Roman roads were regarded with awe by the inhabitants and were thought to have been built by magic. Such constructions were so totally beyond the capabilities of the primitive society which had taken the place of the Roman one that they could not imagine these roads to have been the work of ordinary mortals. The destruction caused by invading bands of Northmen was so extensive that today scarcely anything survives in Britain of the scores of Roman towns which were built during nearly 400 years of Roman occupation. Had we not a comprehensive documentary history of the Roman presence, it would be difficult to realise that Britain was so thoroughly Romanised, if one were to judge by the relative sparseness of archaeological remains alone. The fact that Roman civilisation was so quickly and thoroughly forgotten is more surprising in view of the fact that the continuity of culture was never completely disrupted. Centres of learning survived all the hazards of the Dark Ages both in Britain and Europe, and of course the Renaissance was merely the rediscovery of knowledge which had survived the collapse of the Roman Empire and was brought to light when Constantinople was finally liberated from the Turkish yoke.

The effects of a planetary disaster on a vast scale, with massive geological upheavals and climatic changes, would have been much greater than the disruption caused by the collapse of the Roman Empire, and the scattering of the survivors into small isolated pockets separated by great distances would have hastened the process.

We have perhaps a pointer signifying a great catastrophe in the distant past when we refer to statistics which have been made relating to world populations. It has been estimated that there were some 250 million people 2,000 years ago. In 4800 BC there were 30 million. For 5000 BC the figure is given as 10 million, and in 6000 BC it has been reckoned that there were only 5 million human beings inhabiting the entire planet. At a period some time before 4000 BC the population of Britain was reckoned in the thousands, or even as low as the hundreds, and these in small, scattered groups. It was suggested in *Colony: Earth* that the megalithic complexes in Britain (such as the chambered tombs) were built at this period – prior to 4000 BC – although the archaeologists generally stated at the time that they were built in 1500 BC. Recently these dates have been re-evaluated, and a figure *prior to 4000* BC has been suggested. This remarkable about-face has come about by a re-evaluation of the radio-carbon dating methods. By radio-carbon date-checking against trees of known age – notably the bristlecone pine which grows in the White Mountains of California, some of which are known to be over *6,000 years* old – it has been found that all radio-carbon dates prior to 1000 BC are too young. The date for Stonehenge has also been pushed further back into the past, to 2000 BC, but in the opinion of the author, Stonehenge is really almost as old as the chambered tombs, and should be dated at least a thousand years earlier than even the new period assigned to it.

These new dates will also mean a re-evaluation of the construction methods used to build the megaliths of Western Europe, in view of the small populations involved. It seems obvious that we shall have to seriously reconsider the methods we have suggested for their construction – muscle power by thousands of labourers, who, it now seems, simply did not exist. Let us now set these estimates of small populations in the past, indicating that the entire population was down to a few million 8,000 years ago, against the legends from various parts of the world which point to great populations before the Flood. Genesis in the Bible says 'and mankind spread all over the face of the Earth'. Ancient Sanskrit texts speak of great cities with *60 million* inhabitants being destroyed in one night. The Popol Vuh of the Maya says that 'the lands of the Ten Regions were shaken and torn asunder and the cities with their millions of inhabitants sank beneath the sea'.

Therefore at a point about 8,000 years ago we have stories of populations running into many millions, and soon afterwards populations which are suddenly drastically shrunken. It begins to appear that the idea of tens, or even hundreds, of millions of human beings being killed in an awesome disaster is not so far-fetched. The destruction of the majority of the human race would certainly have thrust those who survived back into a barbarism from which they would have taken centuries to recover. Even the Roman Empire never suffered such a disastrous loss of life as this, and we are all aware how great the dislocation of civilisation this event precipitated, and the centuries that it took for Europe to recover.

It seems that the Ancient Egyptians were aware both of the destruction of former cultures and the setbacks to progress this inevitably caused.

The Egyptian priests told Solon that the destruction of a civilisation by a great calamity would cause that culture's knowledge to be lost. They said that those who would survive would perhaps be rude shepherds guarding their flocks high on mountain tops, while the cities which contained both the knowledge and the scholars would be lost to the fury of the elements. 'You have to begin all over again as children,' a priest told Solon.

In the Timaeus, Plato recorded the words of an Egyptian priest: 'There have been, and there will be again, many destructions of mankind.'

It is perfectly logical to assume that if there had been a nuclear holocaust in the past then the major cities with their huge populations would be the first targets for the weapons. It is in the cities where human knowledge is concentrated – here are the great libraries and universities, and the centres of learning gathered throughout the ages.

In the countryside the simpler people lived, the agriculturalists and guarders of flocks and herds. It seems probable that no matter how advanced a civilisation is, there will always be groups of people who are not concerned with knowledge as such, but who have simpler interests and more mundane pursuits. There is a world of difference between the space scientist and the humble farm labourer – their activities, their knowledge, their outlook and spheres of interest are poles apart, yet they both represent part of the same culture and have the same approximate cultural background. Yet, if you destroy all the scientists and technicians and only leave the farm workers to survive, a civilisation will follow which is much more rural than technological, what technology there is being geared to agricultural activities.

Of course, in a great catastrophe, there will always be some of the intellectuals who would survive, especially in the case of a nuclear or other great catastrophe where there would be advance warning – steps would be taken to ensure that some survived. And that this may have been the case in the world-wide disaster we are discussing, is borne out by two circumstances which have long puzzled scholars. One is the sudden appearance after the Flood of the culture gods, or 'culture-bearers' who led the rude survivors back to civilisation by teaching them the rudiments of building, mathematics, medicine, agriculture, etc. This could indeed have been the outcome of a deliberate policy to ensure educated people survived the catastrophe so that civilisation could be rebuilt. The second is the often uneven way in which some of the ancient civilisations developed. Most of them had the major attributes of civilised living – they built reasonably well-planned cities with proper water supply and drainage, they had organised government, efficient agriculture. Some of them, however, excelled in certain narrow fields – the Maya were the master-mathematicians of the ancient world, the Inca had the most highly organised centralised government, the Chimu possibly the most able surgeons, the Greeks excelled at sculpture and abstract thought. It rather looks as though the culture-bearers were experts in certain fields, so that a certain talent was highly developed in each community that did not occur elsewhere.

10

Further Oddities

There are many things in this world of ours which defy all
the traditional explanations, but which must have an explanation. And if the old answers do not fit, then we must
find new ones, no matter how discomforting to the experts.
A theory is only valid if it fits the facts; new facts are constantly being brought to light which should rightly refute
existing theories, but what was once unorthodox is now dog-
matically accepted, and there is a stubborn refusal to change
even when new evidence ought to make us think anew.

One of the most extraordinary discoveries in recent years
has been made in South America. Dr Daniel Ruzo in 1952
discovered a series of megalithic sculptures at Marcahausi,
some 80 km north-east of Lima in Peru. Marcahausi is a
plateau 4,000 metres above sea level, always cold, and
hardly anything grows in its stony and hostile environment.
What faced Ruzo in a desolate rocky amphitheatre was, by
ordinary accepted standards, unbelievable. There were enormous figures of people carved from the rock, and the faces
displayed the typical features of the main groups of mankind : Mongoloid, Caucasoid and Negroid. There were carvings of lions, elephants, horses, cows and camels. He also
saw a representation of the *amphichelydia*, an extinct ancestor of the turtle known only by fossils.

Most experts are of the opinion that the major influx of
human beings into the Americas was by Mongols who had
filtered across the Bering Strait from Asia some 12,000 years
ago. This would mean that humanity had been occupying
the Americas for only the past 10,000 or 12,000 years. This
concept has been challenged in recent years, as traces of
human beings contemporary with the oldest finds in Europe
have been found, dating back 20,000 or 30,000 years, a discovery which causes heated controversy among anthropolo-

gists. Furthermore, remains of mummified corpses many thousands of years old have been found in Peruvian graves. These have wavy auburn or blond hair, which identifies them as of Caucasoid descent.

The Olmec carvings of giant heads found in Central America have a distinctly negroid cast, although the anthropologists would deny that the Negro ever lived on the American continent until brought there as a slave in recent times.

These carvings, however, show that someone, in the past, knew of these three races; and it is even possible that people of all these types lived at one time in the Americas.

It is known that the horse had been extinct in the Americas for 9,000 years until re-introduced by the Spaniards in the sixteenth century; which fact seems to date the carvings to a very remote period indeed. Analysis of the rock from which the carvings were made confirms a very remote dating, as geologists estimate that the period of time which would be required for the incisions to take on their present greyish tint in the white diorite porphyry would be at least 10,000 years. It would appear, therefore, that the carvings were executed at least 10,000 years ago – about 8000 BC.

There is another curiosity about the sculptures of Marcahausi; some figures can be seen at certain angles of sunlight, while others cannot. The figures change, appear or disappear with the angle of sunlight and shadows. Further, they show different aspects at different times – in one light, one face takes on the appearance of age, at other times it is that of a young man. Obviously, the sculptors had a great deal of knowledge of perspective-drawing and optics.

It seems that we may know the *when* of these strange figures, but we do not know the *who* and the *why*.

A guess can be hazarded as to the who, although we can give no name to the civilisation which vanished so cataclysmically before the dawn of recorded history. Strange optical effects have been noticed in incised carvings from many parts of the world. Many of the monoliths and other megalithic structures in Ireland – New Grange springs to mind – England, and Europe, are carved with spirals, concentric circles and other patterns, some of which can be seen only in certain lights, or at certain times of the day. Sometimes, photographs reveal shapes undetectable to the eye. These optical effects are in many ways reminiscent of those produced by the figures at Marcahausi, and it is not beyond the realms of possibility that the civilisation that carved the one, carved the other. This is not to say that the same people travelled throughout the world executing these works, but that the *same technology was employed*. As the optical carving effects are of wide distribution, they are also another pointer to a world-spanning civilisation at a remote period.

This concept had also occurred to Daniel Ruzo, as he says:

Hundreds of discoveries and observations of this kind made in South America convinced me absolutely that these sculptures could not possibly be mere freaks of nature, but must be the purposive work of a people whose civilisation is as yet unknown. I called it the 'Masma Civilisation'.

All the works of this people had points in common – anthropomorphic and zoomorphic representations, executed within a restricted space, repetitions of the main themes, a combination of different designs on the same piece of rock, the complete effect visible only on a particular date.

Between 1953 and 1958 I sent a number of reports to the Academies of Lima, Mexico and Paris about this.

I observed the same effects in England at Stonehenge and at Avebury, where one of the finest druidic temples in Europe is to be seen. Careful examination of the enormous blocks of stone led me to believe that they had at one time been sculptured.

One can only conclude that certain artists, whose origin is wrapped in mystery, but who were no doubt trained to a kind of four-dimensional form of art, had for thousands of years carried on their function as sculptors for the Masma Civilisation.

Ruzo ends by saying: 'In conclusion, I am of the opinion that in these places we have witness of a vast civilisation that spread over the whole Earth in the days before the

Flood, but which I was unable to analyse in greater detail ...'

The author does not agree on all points with Dr Ruzo, particularly as the Stonehenge and Avebury monuments are far older than any druidic institutions, and although they may have been used by them at a later date, were not built by the Druids. But I do support the view that these sculptures represent but one facet of a highly advanced civilisation from an unknown epoch.

Why were carvings made in South America of animals which no longer live there, to baffle future ages? Was it that all these creatures lived in South America at a remote period, even though we have been unable to trace their fossilised remains? Were these drawings created to show future ages that things were once very different from the present? Perhaps there was another reason. Mount Rushmore in the United States has had a series of gigantic carvings of the heads of American presidents cut into the cliff face. What would future sages, unaware of the history of our civilisation, if it were mysteriously to disappear, make of these monstrous heads? Would they perhaps think they were representations of gods, which they are certainly not, and thus fall into the same trap we have fallen into regarding many aspects of antiquity? Why and how, they may wonder, did these people carve these great images in a remote place, far from a populated centre? Perhaps, at Marcahausi, there was a far more mundane reason for the sculptures.

When these sculptures were new, some 10,000 years ago, it is possible that the climate on the Marcahausi plateau was very different from what it is today. Perhaps it was warm and verdant, in the same way that the present Sahara desert used to be lush grassland swarming with countless animals. Maybe this was merely part of a display in a park which has long since vanished, a park where people could sit and amuse themselves watching the changing lights and shadows alter the figures; or perhaps it was a display in a wildlife reserve, showing the different kinds of animals to be found there. In Hamburg, there is a group of giant concrete figures representing species of dinosaurs in the grounds of the Zoological gardens – it would be interesting to see what experts from the future would make of these if they survived the ravages of time when all else had vanished.

South America contains hundreds of strange enigmatic carvings and markings, some of them huge in scale, which have defied all our scientists' efforts to explain them. Much has been said in recent years about the maze of lines, trapezoids and figures on the Plain of Nazca in Peru, which can only be seen properly *from the air*. Von Daniken (*Chariots of the Gods*) has suggested this area was once an airfield for spacecraft. He suggests that *originally* there were several landing strips laid out either by alien astronauts, or by the primitive inhabitants under the instructions of the aliens; and that the later lines and figures were added by the terrestrial primitives perhaps copying what the 'gods' had made, or making an attempt to signal to them. One feels somewhat uneasy about such a theory. For one thing, it is extremely doubtful whether space vehicles, particularly of the advanced design envisaged for long-duration space flight (Daniken himself suggests that interstellar vehicles would most likely be sphere- or egg-shaped), would need landing strips or runways as they would be more likely to descend and ascend vertically.

The markings of Nazca were discovered from the air – from the ground all that can be seen is a series of white markings against the dark surface, without any discernible pattern. It is a mystery how the figures were created without careful measurements, perhaps a small-scale pattern, and then progress checking *from the air*, as making them from purely a surface view would be almost impossible. The figures are on a vast scale, and very accurate – among the designs can be recognised a monkey, a spider, and several representations of what appear to be humming birds and a condor. It is thus possible that even if all the designs were not made at exactly the same time, they were made by the same technique, which would include *aerial survey*. If some of them were made by advanced methods (Daniken's astronauts) and the others by primitives, there should be an enormous difference in the design ability, but *all* parts are of equal skill. This author suggested in *Colony: Earth* that the pattern may possibly have been an aerial direction indicator, as it seems to bear a resemblance in some of its aspects (particularly the lines themselves) to a string navigational device used by the Polynesians to enable them to find their way across the trackless Pacific.

Indeed, many of the enigmatic markings which exist in South America seem specifically designed to be seen from the air, as either they cannot be seen from the ground, or from surface level they make no sense at all.

In the bay of Paracas, on the coast of Peru, is located the Chandelier of the Miraculous Sign of the Three Crosses. This figure in white on a cliff face looks something like the trident of Neptune with branches, and is 185 ft. high. It has been suggested that it was a guide marker for ships, but because of the enclosed nature of the bay, it can only be seen properly close inshore, which seems to exclude this possibility. A Spanish scholar, Beltran Garcia, has suggested that by pulleys and cords a pendulum could be created using the trident which could record seismic disturbances not only in South America, but anywhere on earth. He thus suggests its purpose as a seismograph. However, the figure can be seen most effectively *from the air*, and perhaps it was really a navigational device of some sort, or even an aerial symbol denoting a national boundary.

Strange markings appear on Andean slopes, resembling parallel lines set closely together, marching across the hills. Their makers and their purpose are quite unknown, and, as with the Nazca lines, can only be detected properly *from the air*.

It remains a mystery but, in some way, the signs must be connected with manned flight in a distant epoch, their true purpose as much hidden from us as many of our symbols of technology would be to a distant future which had forgotten our civilisation.

Of course, the traditionalist will say that there could not have been aircraft in the remote past, that these carvings were made by primitive peoples to appease their celestial gods. But no one has suggested how things like this were created without high-altitude surveys, and no one today would attempt to reproduce such figures from ground level with primitive tools and by rule-of-thumb, because it simply cannot be done!

In the same way, many geologists will say that the light effects on the carvings at Marcahausi occur because of weathering that has taken place during the past few thousand years, and that therefore the effects are accidental. Yet the same effects are seen on stone in Britain and Europe – and, according to Dr Ruzo, in many other parts of the world including Egypt. Surely the effects of all these different climates, different kinds of erosion, some from wind, or sand or water, depending on locality, would not have produced, *accidentally*, identical optical effects? The experts would no doubt deny that the sculptures of horses, lions, etc. from antiquity exist in South America, but there are photographs, *and they are there*, however much the traditionalist may wish them away. New explanations are needed, new answers to old problems.

Much of the working of masonry in antiquity, especially in the Pyramids of Egypt and the megalithic constructions of the Americas, has long baffled the experts. Enormous slabs of walls from Tiahuanacu in Bolivia seem to have been planed absolutely flat, and grooves carved as though with a knife through soft butter. This has led to the idea that perhaps the Inca (or pre-Inca peoples) had some method of softening stone with some sort of chemical so that it could be easily worked, and in support of this it has been suggested that there is a plant in the Amazon basin which exudes an acid which is capable of producing this reaction. However, this has never been verified, nor has it been found to work in practice. It is possible that such a plant does exist, but even if it does there remain other problems unsolved. *How*, in the first place, were such huge masses constructed and erected? It may seem that the *whole* problem of the megaliths could more realistically be solved by assuming the possession of a high technology capable of dealing with *all* the aspects of megalithic construction.

In connection with the actual working of the masonry, it is interesting to note that experiments have been carried out recently in the use of lasers for the purpose of cutting stone. These experiments have been proving successful, and what is more, the effects created are very similar to those of megalithic stone-cutting, even to the glaze produced by the intense heat, which has been observed on some ancient American megalithic structures. We did in fact suggest in *Colony: Earth* that, in view of the fact that no tools have been discovered at many of the ancient sites, and the stone or copper tools which we have assumed to have been used have proved ineffective under modern test conditions, something akin to lasers may have been used by the ancients.

We have seen in our chapter on ancient science that many of our present-day discoveries appear to have been known in antiquity, and there is no reason to think that among their devices may not have been something similar to the laser. At least the proposition offers an explanation both of the apparent ease of stone-cutting and the total lack of tool remains, and of the similarities between the traces on ancient stones and on modern masonry cut by laser. Even if saws had been used in antiquity, it is difficult to imagine the technical difficulties in handling such large slabs by this method, and traces of saw marks should in any case be visible on the stone. Yet, as Verrill remarked in *America's Ancient Civilisations*, the slabs of stone in the wall masonry at Tiahuanacu seemed to have been smoothed absolutely flat as though with a gigantic plane.

Much comment has been aroused recently regarding the stone balls discovered in Costa Rica, Guatemala and Mexico. Their sizes range from some $2\frac{1}{2}$ metres to a few centimetres, and the largest ones weigh 16 tons. Some are set in patterns on platforms, and others are arranged in straight lines or in clusters. They are all perfectly round and polished, and they could hardly have been produced naturally, or we would surely have discovered them in other parts of the world, which we have not. They must be man-made objects, but it seems extremely unlikely that primitive people with almost no tools could have produced such perfectly spherical shapes. The largest globes would have had to be carved from blocks weighing 20 tons or more, and in some cases transported many miles over difficult terrain to the sites where they have been found.

It has been suggested by Robert Charroux in his book

The Mysterious Unkown[1] that when a group of these balls
in Guatemala was arranged into what was considered their
original pattern, they represented the Solar System and the
principal constellations. If this is so, it was a remarkable
feat on the part of the ancients, as it is only within the last
150 years that we have become aware of the true nature of
our planetary system. However, this is not the first evidence
we have come across that there existed in antiquity a great
deal of knowledge regarding the Solar System which was
later forgotten.

In any case, it will be interesting to see what an eventual
survey and accurate mapping of all these stone balls may
bring to light. It is possible that we shall find a parallel between these obviously astronomical arrangements and those
of the megalithic observatories in Europe – perhaps there
was an equivalent of Stonehenge in the Americas.

It is surprising, but even such relatively fragile things as
textiles have survived a great period of time, in some cases
many thousands of years. Even if the actual material has not
survived, the impress of its presence has enabled us to re-
construct its appearance and texture. As with other things,
we have the extraordinary truth emerging that the more
ancient the artifact, the higher its quality. Catal Huyuk in
Anatolian Turkey is one of the oldest cities known to man,
and carpeting has been found there which is of so high a
quality that it compares favourably with those made today.

Prehistoric lake villages, which existed in England and
parts of Europe, have provided us with evidence of a previously unsuspected sophistication. Traces have been found
of a brocaded cloth of a very high standard, which is not a
very easy material to manufacture. It had been thought that
these villages were among the earliest settled communities
only one step removed from nomadic savagery, yet here we
have evidence that they may have been very far from primitive.

In South-West Africa there are rock paintings showing
Bushmen and white women. What is known as the White
Lady of Brandberg shows a white woman with a flower in
her hand. Some have thought these figures depicting white

1. Neville Spearman, 1972.

people represent Cretans or Egyptians who travelled this far south thousands of years ago (the Pharaoh Necho sent an expedition to circumnavigate Africa), but they more resemble Caspians from North Africa who lived there 12,000 years ago. Among the animals painted on the Brandberg rocks, leopards and hippopotami are noticeably absent. It *may* be coincidence but these particular animals did not occupy this region many thousands of years ago, although they do now.

West of Alice Springs, Australia, Michael Terry found a carving of the extinct Nototherium mitchelli on a cliff face. This species had vanished some 2,500 years ago from the Australian continent. Not too extraordinary perhaps – the Australian Aborigine has lived in Australia for many thousands of years – but in the same place were found six representations of what appear to be rams' heads. The most extraordinary drawing, however, was that of a man of European features with a beard, wearing a mitre which closely resembled those of Egyptian or Babylonian design, and drawn in a horizontal position. The ram, and apparently a white man, or at least someone who could have originated in the Middle East, on a rock face in Australia, when the ram was unknown in this region until introduced by European settlers in recent times? Erosion of the rock face which has blurred the carvings hints at their great age. Did people from Europe or the Middle East visit both South-West Africa and Australia in antiquity? But this too is not impossible, especially in view of the Piri Reis map showing Antarctica – if Antarctica was known in ancient times, it is also possible that the countries at 'the bottom of the world' were also known.

A question of interest to every human being from time immemorial is that of health. Even a society sufficiently advanced to have eliminated disease has still to deal with injury by accident. Western society has largely eliminated epidemic disease, but the hospitals contain any number of people who have been injured in various kinds of accidents. Therefore, even if there is no disease, it is necessary to have a thorough knowledge of human anatomy, physiology, and surgical techniques.

We have already mentioned in our chapter on ancient science that a great deal of medical knowledge existed in the past, and that such things as vaccination were foreshadowed thousands of years before Jenner or Pasteur. We have also come across the fact that Ancient Egyptian physicians appear to have been aware of the circulatory system. This fascinating anomaly from a remote period of Egyptian history stems from a single source known as the Edwin Smith Papyrus.

Edwin Smith, a pioneer American Egyptologist, bought the papyrus from a dealer in Luxor in 1862, but as his knowledge of Egyptian was insufficient to translate the technical language of the manuscript, he left it untranslated, and his heirs gave it to the New York Historical Society. It was then translated by the famous Egyptologist J. H. Breasted, with the aid of the distinguished physician Arno B. Luckhardt.

The papyrus dates back to the Egyptian Old Kingdom (*circa* 3000 BC). Egyptian civilisation is reckoned to be older than this, and the nature of the text of the Smith Papyrus suggests that this document is in fact a copy of the original: the writer seems not to be familiar with some of the technical terms he is copying (or translating?), as he interposes explanations, which have led to the assumption that the copyist was not one versed in medical or surgical techniques.

The papyrus is, however, a remarkable document in that unlike much of Egyptian medical texts which have survived, it is completely devoid of supernatural overtones and religio-magical practices, being thoroughly rational and scientific.

The Smith Papyrus was apparently intended to be a complete review of surgical techniques, and it may have constituted a small fraction of a complete encyclopedia of medicine and surgery. The part we have in our possession is limited to surgical matters connected with the head, arms and chest. It lists 48 surgical cases, mostly injuries: 27 to the head, 6 to the throat and neck, 2 to the clavicle, 3 to the humerus and 8 were chest cases, including tumours and abscesses.

The injuries are described in detail, each under a heading 'Instructions', as in the following example: 'Instructions concerning a gaping wound in his head, penetrating to the bone and splitting his skull.' The 'Examination' then details the interrogation of the patient, inspection, palpation and execution of movements under the direction of the surgeon. In the 'Diagnosis', the physician lists the three possibilities open to him: 'An ailment which I will treat' (curable), 'An ailment with which I will contend' (possibly curable, perhaps fatal, but treatment will be attempted) and 'An ailment not to be treated' (a serious case with a possibly fatal outcome for which the surgeon would not accept responsibility).

This papyrus is the first document in recorded history to mention the word 'brain', whose convolutions are likened to the corrugations formed on cooling slag from molten copper. The pulsations of the brain under the surgeon's exploring fingers when it is exposed are likened to 'the throbbings and flutterings under the fingers like the weak place of an infant's crown before it becomes whole'. The meninges and the contained cerebrospinal fluid, the sutures of the skull and other skeletal details are mentioned and described in clinical fashion.

The physicians who originated the papyrus were aware of the pulse and its significance in indicating the patient's state of health. Its observation, they said, was 'like measuring the ailment of a man' and they were aware that the heart was the organ responsible for the pulsating vessels in all parts of the body – something which was not to be known again for another 5,000 years when William Harvey demonstrated the circulatory system in 1628.

The physicians of this remote time had a thoroughly modern approach to brain injuries and their effects. They were aware of paralysis of the extremities by injuries to the brain, and knew which side of the body would be affected by an injury to a certain side of the brain. They also knew that the left hemisphere of the brain controlled the right-side motor movements and vice-versa. Unlike many other ancient cultures, the Egyptians of the Smith Papyrus did not use trephination in the treatment of skull injuries. Soft tissue wounds were treated with sutures or adhesive tape, splints and bandages were applied as today. It was noted that skull fractures were frequently accompanied by bleeding from the ears and nostrils. In fractures of the midcervical vertebrae, priapism, seminal emission and involuntary urination were all noted, with emphasis on the extremely unfavourable prognosis.

It has been said that this first recorded surgical treatise still makes very good, sound reading for modern surgeons.

The Edwin Smith Papyrus is unlike any other medical text in antiquity, and for this early period of Egyptian history it is unique. The knowledge it displays of the small section of the human anatomy described is so exact and modern that, if it is true that it is only a part of a larger work, ancient knowledge on surgical, and possibly also medical, matters may have been as extensive as that we possess today. It must seem obvious that this knowledge did not spring from Ancient Egyptian civilisation as such, but must have been *inherited from an earlier time*. In this respect it is comparable to the ancient maps, which are themselves fragments of a larger whole and as advanced as modern charts, and the Antikythera Computer, which also could have stemmed from the archaic Greek civilisation.

We would suggest that the Smith Papyrus is only a fragment, which happens to have survived, of the recorded knowledge once stored in the Pyramids by an advanced civilisation of remote times. Possibly the complete copy was contained within the great library of Alexandria, and this fragment, by a fluke, escaped destruction either by not being in the library when it was destroyed, or because it is a copy from elsewhere.

We have already mentioned that the Greeks obtained most of their knowledge from Egypt, and this is true of medical matters. The Father of Medicine, Hippocrates, was born in 460 BC, and the more than seventy books called the Corpus Hippocraticum attributed to him were probably in fact a team effort by his followers and students. The grasp of surgical matter displayed by Hippocrates is remarkable, and in the matter of dislocations particularly, his knowledge was *more extensive* than that possessed by many modern surgeons, unless they specialise in orthopaedics. Special deformities were discussed and clubfoot treatment by non-operative techniques described in great detail. Two common modern conditions, bladder stone and hernia, are almost the only two conditions not mentioned in the Hippocratic texts, though it is possible that these have been lost. Hippocrates and his followers travelled widely and studied over a large area. Some of their observations, methods of treatment, diagnoses and prognoses are so similar to those in the Smith Papyrus that it could be reasonably inferred that much of their knowledge was gathered from it and other scrolls of ancient wisdom held in the great libraries of Egypt.

Leonardo da Vinci has been hailed as the most complete all-round genius in history, a man '500 years ahead of his time'.

He invented many things: a water filtration plant, helicopter, aircraft, many novel weapons of war and new forms of cannon, as well as being a writer and artist. He seemed fascinated by the secrets of flight, as his many extant drawings show. Recently, a formerly unknown drawing by da Vinci has been discovered, showing in graphic detail a *Lunar landing*. Should we not wonder: where did he obtain the remarkable inspiration for this, and possibly other things? Was he the matchless genius we have always thought? Or did he, perhaps, have access to ancient and secret texts and plans which showed aircraft and space travel? These things are recorded in mythology. Perhaps somewhere there also existed more concrete evidence than awed myths of a vanished age: actual texts, technical information and drawings, plans and designs. Of course, da Vinci could not put any of these things to practical use – the technology just did not exist in his age to enable such things as aircraft to be constructed. Possibly some of these documents and drawings may still exist somewhere, hidden away from prying eyes and from those who would destroy them, and now long forgotten? In this case da Vinci, if ancient texts were really his inspiration, would not, even if he wanted to, be able to proclaim publicly the source of his genius. Ancient texts from pre-Christian times, were, in the mental Dark Ages of Europe, hunted down, hidden or burned by the zealots of the Catholic Church, and frequently their owners were likewise hunted and burned as traffickers with the Devil.

Much knowledge from a remote and vanished civilisation

may have survived the wars, ignorance and disorders of the pre-Classical and Classical world, only to have been destroyed by the mindless superstitions of the early Christian world. From the fragments that survive, only now may we guess at the enormity of our loss.

11

The Myths of Our Time

Our history has been grossly distorted: to anyone with an open mind, this must by now be obvious. A new appraisal of the past should be made, and it will no doubt be found that our history books, especially those relating to the more distant eras, will have to be re-written. The same old, tired, hackneyed things are still being taught in our schools and universities, and new discoveries are ignored or glossed over – a state of affairs which cannot last indefinitely.

Not all the blame can be laid at the doors of our teachers, experts and professors. Too often a new approach to the past of the human race has been easily dismissed or ignored as outrageous or 'cranky' because it has been presented in a manner that, to this author, is quite frankly unreal, or at worst downright nonsensical.

Most scholars refuse to associate themselves, for example, with the Atlantis problem, and quite rightly. Possibly no subject on earth has led to so much speculation, theorising and plain idiocy. People have expanded the allusions to Atlantis in the writings of Plato into an entire mythology of a vanished island (or continent) complete with all the gadgetry of super-science and a master-race of geniuses. Why this should be so, it is hard to say – possibly much of the motivation is wish-fulfilment, and a little may be a real recognition that there could have existed in the past a highly advanced civilisation which was completely destroyed. But the mistake has been to associate this idea with Plato's *Atlantis*. Plato, in his dialogues, could not have been plainer. He was describing a civilisation of the Aegean world: he mentions chariots, bowmen, spearmen, the style of buildings and temples which were a familiar part of the Mediterranean world for at least 2,000 years up to the beginning of the Christian era. Since then, Atlantis has been placed in nearly every region on the face of the Earth, and every archaeological curiosity has been credited to the mysterious Atlanteans.

There are those who will say that Plato reduced Atlantis to terms familiar to him in his day, and that he merely rendered a 'Greek' version of the story handed to him by his ancestor Solon. There is no evidence to support this. However much people want to disbelieve it, I believe that the Atlantis problem has been solved – is is explained by the volcanic destruction of Thera (Santorini) and the consequent destruction of the Cretan Sea Empire in 1500 BC. Yet the myth is still being perpetuated. We do not even need Plato's story to solve the mysteries of our past. There are threads which lead to another, infinitely more ancient civilisation than the Atlantis of Plato, to which however we can give no name, since no name has come down to us.

Possibly, it never had a name, as such, in the same way that our civilisation, as a culture, has no name. We have what we describe as our twentieth-century technological civilisation; it is not specifically English, or American, German, or Japanese, or Russian. It is a *condition* which has spread over the entire planet. The same situation may have arisen in the past – the endless duplication of legends from all over the world about a vanished Golden Age points to this fact. If our civilisation were to vanish in a gigantic holocaust, a similar series of legends may arise – and they also would be of world-wide distribution – *because the civilisation which gave them birth was of world-wide distribution.*

Hand in hand with the Atlantis theories goes another myth of a super-civilisation, based on the other side of the world – the vanished Pacific continent of Lemuria or Mu.

Lemuria commenced its life as a scientific hypothesis to explain the existence of lemurs, those small animals which are regarded as the most primitive representatives of the primate family. Lemurs live mainly in Madagascar, but they are also distributed through Africa and tropical Asia.

William T. Blandford suggested that there may once have been a land-bridge connecting Southern Africa and India. This idea was used by the German biologist, Ernst Heinrich Haeckel, who suggested that this land-bridge was the method by which the lemurs populated the various continents during the Cenozoic (Age of Mammals) which began some seventy million years ago.

This concept of land-bridges connecting continents was seized upon by some people, especially the occultists, and expanded into a theory of continents populated by various advanced races.

Possibly the most famous exponent of the lost continent of Lemuria idea was the founder of the Theosophist movement, Madame Blavatsky, who included it in her weird cosmology. She also incorporated Atlantis, an imaginary continent based on ancient Greek allusions to the Land of the Hyperboreans, which she called Hyperborea, situated in the Arctic.

Mu is derived from Churchward, who thought that the Maya civilisation in Yucatan was a fragment of a sunken continent called Mu. The name Mu is based on a supposed translation of the two Maya glyphs regarding a tradition about the Flood, but as no Maya glyphs apart from numerical ones have ever been translated, there is no certainty that the Maya ever actually called anywhere 'Mu'. The Popol Vuh *does* refer to the Flood and the destruction of the First Men, and the Mexicans refer also to a great catastrophe and to the Dead Lands to the North. However, there is no reference to sunken continents as such.

The geography of the Pacific would seem to exclude the possibility that there ever existed a continental mass which sank – at least not within human times, although there may have existed different land areas many hundreds of millions of years ago. The same thing applies to the Atlantic Ocean region, where both oceanographers and geologists are agreed that no large land area could have existed within geologically recent times. The discovery of land-created lava from the bed of the Atlantic has sometimes been cited as proof that there did exist a continent or huge island in the Atlantic, but of course it is possible that a *small* volcanic island vanished beneath the waves. It is exceedingly doubtful whether a large land mass could have sunk beneath the Atlantic, particularly within the last ten thousand years, without leaving noticeable traces for the geologists.

Although the Atlantis theory is still strongly advanced,

with new locations constantly being offered, the Pacific continent has largely fallen from favour, although occasionally it is brought into the light of day. The arguments put forward in its favour centre largely around the mysterious giant statues of Easter Island, and the lagoon city of Nan Matol on Ponape in the Carolines. Here, the pro-Mu or Lemuria theorists say, is proof of a vanished continent. These mysteries stem from Mu (or Lemuria), being the last visible remnants – the part that did not disappear beneath the waves.

Easter Island, it is true, does pose a riddle which has never been resolved. Apart from the enormous number of huge statues (the great heads actually have bodies, rather small in proportion to the heads, buried in the ground), there have been found a number of tablets inscribed with a great number of symbols which appear to be some form of writing. The inscriptions on these tablets have never been deciphered.

It would seem that Thor Heyerdahl's explanation of the statues is the most reasonable – that they have a connection with one of the cultures of the Peru/Bolivia region. There are certain similarities between them and the megalithic statues of Tiahuanacu on the shores of Lake Titicaca in Bolivia. However, the faces at Tiahuanacu are completely different from those of Easter Island – the heads of Tiahuanacu are square and stylised, whilst those of Easter Island are long, with sunken eye-sockets and long noses. Similarities do exist – both groups wear stone 'hats', and the Easter Island statues have long ears, similar to the 'Long Ears' noted by the Spaniards among the ruling elite of the Inca of Peru. No writing in South America has ever been found which is comparable with the Easter Island script. But on the other hand no direct connection has been found between Easter Island script and the statues – those who carved the statues may not have written the tablets.

Apart from Thor Heyerdahl, no one has offered any satisfactory archaeological explanation for the vast number of huge statues on Easter Island, as it is a small and bleak place which cannot support a large population. One would have thought that an army of workmen would have been needed to carve and move these statues from their quarries to the hillsides where they were set up, to say nothing of the numbers of ancillary people such as food-suppliers, house-builders, etc., and the attendant women and children. Easter Island simply could not ever have supported such numbers.

Another writer, Erich von Daniken, has suggested that spacemen were marooned on the island and built the statues with the aid of their own technology, either as a signal, or simply to while away the time awaiting rescue. This would account, he says, for the number of unfinished statues still lying there – as soon as the rescuers came, the spacemen dropped what they were doing and went away into the sky. Hence the island's other name, 'The Island of the Birdmen'. Incidentally, it also has a Polynesian name, 'The Navel of the World'.

It does seem unlikely, not to say ludicrous, that a group of spacemen marooned temporarily on an alien planet would spend their time building a vast number of great statues, all the same, and setting them up all over the hillsides. It seems very doubtful if representatives from an advanced technological civilisation would go to such lengths merely to pass the time, and as signals they would probably have more sophisticated methods, such as a directional radio beacon.

The mystery of Easter Island, therefore, remains, and is likely to cause a great deal of controversy for many years to come.

Nan Matol on Ponape is an even more unlikely candidate for identification as the remains of a highly advanced civilisation.

There is a broad bay in the south-eastern end of Ponape, and the ruins of Nan Matol are situated on a small island called Temuen, which, at high tide, is broken up into almost a hundred tiny islets. Most of the islets are surrounded by huge walls, 30 ft. high. At high tide, the 11 square miles of Nan Matol appears like some ruined Venice.

The walls and all the buildings are built of a dark blue prismatic basalt, a similar-appearing rock to that which forms the Giant's Causeway in Ireland. It appears that the builders of Nan Matol obtained their materials from the island of Jokaz, off the northern coast of Ponape, and rafted them fifteen miles around the island to the site. Prisms scattered along the sea bottom on the route show where some of these rafts must have sunk with their loads.

The six-sided lengths of prismatic basalt were laid in alternate courses in the wall, rather after the fashion of a log cabin. The operation is crudely executed, for there are numerous holes and no attempt had been made to dress the stone or ensure a close-fitting coherent mass.

The ruins are impressive nevertheless, especially when seen from a distance. But it could not possibly be suggested that they were the handiwork of an advanced civilisation. No statuary has been found, and no inscriptions of any sort have ever been discovered within the precincts of the complex. Careful sifting through the legends of the Ponapeans, together with analysis by radio-carbon methods, has now produced the estimate that Nan Matol was built in approximately AD 1400 – or rather from AD 1400 onwards, since it was added to by successive kings, who had the title of Satalur. There are the remains of the king's house, priests' quarters, temples and altars: the place was apparently a cult centre connected with the worship of the Sacred Turtle. There is no possibility that this place was a remnant of a highly advanced civilisation called Lemuria which sank beneath the Pacific. Even so, no doubt someone, at some time or other, will attempt to revive the theory of a sunken continent in the Pacific, in the same way that the Atlantis myth is being constantly resurrected in differing forms.

Many people have reported from time to time sightings of ruins or outlines of buildings in shallow coastal waters. An aircraft during the war claimed, according to its observer, seeing the outlines of huge buildings in shallow water off the Pacific coast of South America. Divers have claimed to have seen submerged buildings in the Gulf of Mexico, and there are reports that the bed of the Arctic Ocean is littered with the remains of a submerged forest.

It has been said that during the last Ice Age so much water may have been locked within the ice fields that the ocean levels may have been lower than they are today, and that extensive areas of the continental shelves could have been inhabited. When the ice melted, these areas were flooded as the oceans rose to their present levels, and the inhabited areas were abandoned. This is one explanation for the possible existence of ruins in shallow offshore waters.

Alternatively, as was suggested in *Colony: Earth*, there may have been no Ice Age, but a warmer climate, which would still have meant a lowering of the ocean levels as a result of a higher rate of evaporation of surface water. The sudden lowering of temperatures would have caused excessive precipitation, creating the same effect as the melting of the hypothetical ice fields – a rise in ocean levels.

However, even this hypothesis is open to question, and it is possible that there was actually no lowering of ocean levels within human times. The ancient maps previously referred to certainly offer no evidence of such a process. These maps show both the South and North Polar regions without the ice; yet they show all the continental outlines *as they are today*, and similarly the distances between continental masses, all of which are accurately charted. They therefore appear to show a world devoid of ice, which is in opposition to the Ice Age theory; yet they do not show any lowering of ocean levels to expose any of the continental shelves.

Indeed, even if the planet had been warmer, which would have meant increased evaporation, there could also have been increased precipitation of water – in other words, a warmer, but perhaps slightly wetter world, which would have maintained the ocean levels at a constant similar to that existing today. The fact that many thousands of years ago all our deserts were fertile areas would also seem to point to a warmer but wetter world.

How then do we explain the buildings seen – or claimed to have been seen – in offshore waters? There are two possible explanations. Possibly they do not exist, and what have been seen are natural formations. The Giant's Causeway is a natural formation, but the rock formations are so regular as almost to appear to be artificial. Submerged prismatic basaltic formations could similarly be mistaken for artificial constructions. Alternatively, the remains of buildings, and the trunks of trees which litter the bed of the Arctic Ocean, *could* have found their way to these locations during the enormous disturbances created by the Flood Catastrophe. Tremendous gales and tidal waves could have wrenched coastal buildings and vegetation and carried them to shallow waters surrounding the coasts.

Of course there is always the possibility that there were buildings in what is now coastal waters, and it may be true that the Arctic and North Sea were once dry land, and that England was joined to the continent of Europe. We would then have to explain away the ancient Maps of Piri Reis, which show continental outlines with great accuracy, including the ice-free polar regions, with the ocean levels apparently the same as they are today. Conceivably the maps were drawn up to show the dispositions of land and sea *after* the catastrophe, but before the ice caps had formed in their present locations. Alternatively, the maps may have been based on charts when the ocean levels were lower, but altered to show the newer levels as navigational aids in the period following the changed state of the world.

However, it is beginning to look as though there may never have been any sunken lands occupied by the human race – not of any consequence at any rate, and not during the past thirty or forty thousand years.

The unknown civilisation which vanished before the dawn of recorded history may in fact have occupied similar areas to those today, but including once ice-free polar regions at present virtually uninhabitable.

We have attempted to show, in this volume, that there may have existed in the remote past a highly advanced civilisation which was destroyed in a vast catastrophe, possibly intelligently engineered. There exists the distinct possibility of a nuclear holocaust in the past. This disaster may have been limited to this planet, or it may have involved three, or possibly four inhabited planets within this Solar System, one of which was completely shattered by weapons of frightful power, and whose fragments scarred the other inner planets. Both nuclear weapons used on Earth, and bombardment by fragments of a shattered world, may have been responsible for the destruction of the civilisation and the shift in the Earth's axial and orbital position. There is a possibility that there used to be a planet where the asteroid belt is now situated. The scarred condition of the inner planets and the Moon, the discovery of glass 'marbles' and glassy areas on the Moon, and the existence of tektites on Earth, all of which could have been formed by the intense flash heat of nuclear reactions, point to the possibility of a sustained artificially-engineered chain reaction which destroyed a planet.

Such a possibility would fit in with some of the Old Testament statements about the heavens being shaken and the Earth being moved out of her place. It would also fit with some sections of the Apocalypse in Revelations, which describe the War in Heaven. In one place indeed it is said that a great star fell to Earth.

It would appear that much of Revelations is concerned with destruction, and much of the writing, and the psychological background which underlies it, is connected with the great Thera volcanic eruption, which caused such havoc in the second millennium BC and left a traumatic shock of such magnitude among all the peoples in the region of the crowded Eastern Mediterranean that it possibly took them centuries to recover. However, there are also echoes of earlier disasters and conflicts which would seem to have been telescoped into a generalised series of disasters which in turn have been stylised into a religiously-orientated Nemesis.

The Bible, and particularly the Old Testament, has been subjected to a great deal of scrutiny in recent years, and highly popular at the present time is an attempt to identify certain Biblical phenomena with the activities of visitors from other worlds. It may be that there is a danger of reading too much into Biblical writings – many parts of the Old Testament are so ambiguously written that almost anything may be translated or interpreted out of them.

On the other hand there is no doubt that some things in the Old Testament can be associated with the phenomena we today describe as UFOs – particularly the episode of Moses on the Mount (although as Exodus too is closely linked with the Thera eruption, this could also be connected with vulcanism), and the episode of Ezekiel which has strong parallels with present-day UFO reports.

However, it remains true to say that a great many gaudy, unreal and impossible cosmic fantasies have been evolved both around Biblical passages, and around the legends about Atlantis, Lemuria and Hyperborea. How people can create complete continents populated by advanced civilisations out of almost nothing, is incredible. The Greeks for instance mentioned a land, or rather an island, called Hyperborea, beyond where the North Wind blows, where there was a round temple dedicated to Apollo, and whose inhabitants were favourably disposed towards the Greeks. Yet there is not the slightest necessity to invent an entire new continent out of this Greek legend. Like most legends, it has within it a core of truth for which a quite reasonable hypothesis can be made without inventing further vanished continents.

The region obviously refers to somewhere far north of the Greeks, which could mean the British Isles or Scandinavia. However, the fact that it is mentioned as an island where there was a round temple, would seem to narrow it down to the British Isles and Stonehenge (the Round Temple). The reference to Apollo is interesting, as it may be that there is a distinct connection between Apollo of the Greeks and the reason for an ancient name for Britain – Merlin's Enclosure. There has arisen a certain degree of confusion about the name Merlin (the magician of King Arthur's court), for he has also been associated with far more ancient monuments, such as Stonehenge. It is thought by some mythographers that the name Merlin's Enclosure is a corruption of an even more ancient name: a Welsh triad says that before men came to the British islands they were called 'Clas Myrddin' – and Myrddin was an ancient Celtic Sky God. Apollo, as a celestial deity of the Greeks, could be related to the Celtic Myrddin. It was said in Greek mythology that Leto, the mother of Apollo, was born on the island of the Hyper-boreans, and that the priests of the island were regarded (by the Greeks) as priests of Apollo. One is tempted to wonder whether the relationship between Myrddin and Apollo was even closer – could they in fact have been aspects, under different names, of the same celestial deity?

It is also interesting to note that the Greeks said that on visits to the Hyperboreans they left gifts and votive offerings inscribed in Greek – and at Stonehenge there are representations of Greek swords and Greek lettering carved on the columns. This has led to the theory being advanced that Greek mathematicians or travelling architects and builders were responsible for the construction of Stonehenge. But it now begins to appear that the truth was actually the other way round – in fact the Greeks came to Stonehenge to *learn* from the builders, who were the mysterious Hyperboreans. We remember at this point the Antikythera Computer, and our suggestion that this may have originated from the Stonehenge mathematicians in Britain – and this not only strengthens the Greek ties with the Hyperboreans, but makes the Greeks the students and the Hyperboreans the builders and teachers.

It must be obvious that a close study of the Greek legends regarding the land of the Hyperboreans identifies it more closely with Britain than with any other area – all the facts, derived both from mythology and from the discoveries of actual physical remains, particularly in the area of Stonehenge, would seem to suggest that the Island of the Hyperboreans was actually Britain. The invention of a sunken or otherwise vanished mythical continent situated in the present Polar regions is not only necessary, it is absurd.

It is remarkable how a vast *modern mythology* has arisen out of two Greek legends, both obviously based on fact. Atlantis and Hyperborea have been the subject of an endless series of speculations and theories, and each has been used to explain a great many of the mysteries of the past.

Much of the blame for the modern mythology regarding Atlantis, Lemuria and Hyperborea can be placed at the door of someone we have already mentioned – Madame Blavatsky. Although she has been largely forgotten by the public at large and her rambling, nonsensical universe dismissed for the fabrication it obviously is, her influence obviously remains strong among certain of the modern writers engaged in speculation about the past.

Briefly, the Blavatsky universe, described in her monumental Theosophist work *The Secret Doctrine*, was revealed to her in a trance by means of an Atlantean 'history', the Book of Dyzan. There were different 'Root Races', the first being a sort of invisible jellyfish, who lived in the Imperishable Sacred Land. The Second Root Race lived in Hyperborea, which was situated in the Arctic and broke up. Following the destruction of Hyperborea, Lemuria formed in the Southern Hemisphere, and was inhabited by the Third Root Race, giant apelike creatures with four arms and sometimes with eyes in the backs of their heads. Lemuria in turn sank beneath the sea, and its place was taken (in the North Atlantic, however) by Atlantis, inhabited by the highly advanced Atlanteans, the Fourth Root Race. We today, following the destruction of Atlantis and the development of the present-day land masses, are the Fifth Root Race. It appears that the Sixth Root Race, to follow this, will evolve from present-day North America, and the Seventh (and final) Root Race, will emerge from South America. One wonders why she did not invent some new continent to emerge like some watery phoenix from the depths of the ocean!

This farrago of ill-conceived nonsense was based on several sources: the Greek writings of Atlantis, extant in the Criteas of Plato; the widely known legend of the Island of the Hyperboreans; Donelly's monumental *Atlantis*, and the many occult works of the late nineteenth century. The 'Book of Dyzan' was cribbed from the 'Hymn of Creation' in the Sanskrit Rig-Veda, and Lemuria from the hypothetical land-bridge and Churchward's Mu of the Mayas.

It is difficult to understand how anyone could be taken in by this patently unreal 'history' of the world, yet some modern writers appear to have 're-discovered' *The Secret Doctrine*, and evolved new theories based on the Blavatsky thesis.

Robert Charroux, a French writer, appears to have based many of his ideas on the writings of Blavatsky, and particularly on *The Secret Doctrine*. He has also been influenced by a curious so-called legend regarding the founding of the city of Tiahuanaco in Bolivia. This legend has it that Tiahuanaco was founded by a woman called Orejona, who landed in a golden spaceship near Lake Titicaca and gave birth to the human race by mating with (of all things) a tapir! This particular legend is not one which figures in any of the traditions of the Andean peoples, either Inca or any of their forerunners, but it was reported by Bertan Garcia, who claims he saw it in a secret manuscript belonging to the historian Garcilaso de la Vega – but this manuscript has never been seen. The legend would seem therefore to be rather the work of someone's imagination, and is of sixteenth-century origin.

As Peter Kolosimo says in his book *Not of This World*, Chapter Two: 'The Devils From Space':

> It is depressing to see how Charroux, a writer who is certainly not rigidly scientific but at least appreciated by some for his brilliant deductions, has sunk down to the histrionic level of Adamski. And it is still more melancholy to note that this is the end of many an investigator who, having seriously approached unusual problems, falls for the charms of crude theories, queer associations of ideas and interpretations. Thus they compromise themselves as they are unable to withdraw from the positions they take up and end by having to resort to distortions and falsehoods.
>
> Apart from discrediting themselves, they obviously increase the destructive and slanderous effect which the champions of orthodox scientific conservatism have on the genuine students who are engaged in revolutionary research.

This writer agrees wholeheartedly with this sentiment. I referred earlier in this book to the fact that the 'lunatic fringe' automatically brings the scorn of the orthodox down on the heads of those who suggest a new approach.

Charroux, in his distortion of the Blavatsky doctrine, sees the descendants of the vanished continent of Hyperborea as the Celts, who were responsible for the civilisations of the Mexican and Middle American races. He claims, in effect, that the ancestors of the Aztecs and Mayas were Celts from Northern Europe, and that they are in fact latter-day Hyperboreans. A similar line of reasoning was adopted by Beaumont in his book *The Riddle of Prehistoric Britain*, where he also stated that it was his opinion that the Aztecs were descended from Celtic immigrants in pre-history.

To a rather smaller extent, von Daniken (*Chariots of the Gods*) appears to have been influenced by *The Secret Doctrine*, as he quotes this as one of his source materials, and also appears to take some of the peculiar ideas expressed there with some seriousness.

What is disturbing is the thought that the day may come when any one of these curious theories about sunken continents may be given a ring of authenticity by an established orthodox figure, who *may* decide at some future time to support the contention that such a continent existed. Perhaps, in some time to come, it may be written into the textbooks that there existed a continent in the North Atlantic called Atlantis from which the civilisations of the Old and New Worlds were descended. Selective evidence, especially in view of the many new discoveries made since the end of World War II, could advance a very plausible case for such a continent, and it could be argued that this is the most likely theory to fit the facts to hand.

This is not fantasy, neither is it completely unlikely; it has happened before on more than one occasion.

We have the theory of Evolution, about which so much has been written, and which is propagated with such enthusiasm in every school and university *in the world*, that most people believe it is an actual, demonstrable *fact*. This it is certainly not. It is a *theory*, created by orthodox science to oppose the (to the scientific mind) unacceptable concept of Divine Creation. The theory is composed of scattered evidence, most of which is not very tenable, and a mass of often contradictory suppositions. One famous biologist has said that 'we believe in Evolution, not so much because it is true, but because it is the only alternative we have to Divine Creation'.

We also have the theory of the Ice Ages, again about which numberless volumes have been written, and which is likewise taught in every school and university. Again, almost everyone believes this to be the absolute truth, demonstrable in every aspect. Again, it is merely a theory, created to explain certain biological and geographical peculiarities, for which there are alternative explanations which are equally valid. The causes of the Ice Ages are vaguely stated, hedged about with innumerable difficulties; and for the warmer conditions of the Climatic Optimum, which was supposed to have followed the last, Pleistocene Ice Age, there does not even exist a hint of a theory, let alone an explanation.

These two concepts alone are based on evidence almost as flimsy as the evidence for the Atlantic Atlantis or the Lemurian Land Bridge.

It is stated here that we do not need any of these theories to explain the development of our planet and its inhabitants. We need neither a theory of human evolution, nor a hypothetical ice age, nor an infinite number of mythical or sunken continents.

We have suggested that this planet could have been colonised from other solar systems. This is not impossible; no doubt we ourselves will do this at some time in the future. What we will one day be capable of doing, other races before us may have done. More than one planet in this system may have been inhabited in times long past; the colonists from other planetary systems may have developed powerful civilisations with space travel and the nuclear apparatus of their own destruction. Possibly this event occurred in the unwritten past, leaving legends of catastrophic events on Earth and in the heavens which would explain many strange aspects of mythology, such as the anger of God and the War in Heaven.

Such a war, waged on an interplanetary scale, will, within the forseeable future, be possible. What may our remote, primitive descendants make of the stories of such events? Will they not perhaps devise a mythology which closely resembles that which we ourselves possess today?

Such a conflict in the remote past would not only explain the curious legends which exist; it would also explain many other aspects of our past.

It would explain the existence of areas of scientific knowledge which must have stemmed from an era of technology and instrumentation.

It would explain the sudden emergence of civilisation around 4000 BC: civilisations in many parts of the world appear to have sprung into existence fully formed, and this points to the survival of knowledge from an earlier time.

We do lack, at the present time, *absolute* proof that such a superior civilisation existed. Why, we are asked, if such a civilisation existed, have we not by now discovered the remains of some machine, parts of a computer, or an aircraft, or even the rusted remains of a rifle?

There are two principal answers to this question. One is that an artifact of this nature may one day be found – we have simply not found one as yet. On the other hand, the science of a past civilisation may have developed along such different paths from ours that we would not recognise the artifacts even if we found them. One could consider the case of the rocks found in Virginian (USA) woods around which nothing will grow. It is a curious thing, but no trees have ever been known to grow in the vicinity of Stonehenge. In the fifty-six 'Aubrey Holes' which comprise the outer perimeter of the monument there are small pieces of bluestone. The purpose of these small fragments is completely unknown. What if these stones had been impregnated with some substance, or had their molecular structure altered in some way (perhaps to emit a certain spectrum of radiation we cannot detect, or a certain wavelength of vibration), which inhibits plant growth?

What we would then have is an artifact, something which has been intelligently altered to fulfil a specific purpose : any object thus functioning is, properly speaking, a machine. Such rocks, therefore, fulfil the purpose of machines, which we are completely unable to recognise. Our definition of technology is an artifact of machined parts, operated from a linked power-source, and manifestly artificial in its appearance. The fact that an object which fulfils the purpose of a machine looks like a piece of rough-hewn stone does not make it any less a machine. It is merely our definition of technology that is limited.

The other factor is that machines as we understand the term are extremely unlikely to survive for thousands of years. It is extremely doubtful if any of our machines – an automobile, say, or an aircraft or TV set – would survive for very long in a world totally reverted to savagery. No doubt those things which did not rust away and dissolve back into the ground would be broken up and their metals melted down for use as weapons, etc. There is a case in point. In the grave of a Chinese general – that of Chow Chu (AD 265–316) – was discovered a metal girdle made of aluminium. This metal is extremely difficult to refine and process from its ore – bauxite – and requires the resources of a complex technology. It would appear that such a technology did not exist in China at this time. We remember that in Chinese legends there are reports of aircraft, as there were in old Indian sagas. What if this belt were re-fashioned from the parts of one such ancient aircraft, found perhaps decaying and rotting away, its true function, purpose and shape already unrecognisable and unknown? It is not entirely impossible.

More delicate artifacts, such as the fine wiring and circuitry of something akin to our own electronics, would be unlikely to survive for many years, let alone the centuries or millennia which have elapsed since our hypothetical civilisation passed away.

No doubt future sages would be hard put to it to explain their theories of an advanced civilisation from our period, in view of the paucity of physical remains – it is extremely doubtful if any of our artifacts of an advanced nature would survive a disastrous nuclear holocaust and thousands of years of savagery.

Yet one thing is certain – the present-held view of the origin and development of civilisation, and even of man himself, does not ring entirely true. There exist too many anomalies, too many things which should not exist, both in our mythologies, and in our areas of knowledge, for man to have advanced from barbarism only during the past few thousand years. There are also many physical remains which point to a different state of affairs – the Pyramids, Stonehenge and the other megaliths, the megalithic walls of Peru, and, at the other end of the scale, minute artifacts which do not seem to have been capable of manufacture without the aid of sophisticated techniques.

The future will show which point of view is the correct one. One day will be discovered a document, or an artifact, which will prove, beyond a doubt, that mankind and all his works were once almost completely destroyed in a vast holocaust. Until that day arrives, we must open our minds and formulate bolder theories, and continue the search. The answers we seek may be buried in the ground under our feet, or far away among the beckoning stars.

MYSTERIES OF THE UNIVERSE – REVEALED

Pauwels & Bergier

Eternal Man	£1.25 ☐
Planet of Impossible Possibilities	£1.25 ☐
The Morning of the Magicians	£1.25 ☐

Guy Lyon Playfair

The Unknown Power	95p ☐
The Indefinite Boundary	95p ☐

Brinsley Le Poer Trench

Secret of the Ages	60p ☐

Eric & Craig Umland

Mystery of the Ancients	50p ☐

Jacques Vallee

UFOs: The Psychic Solution	85p ☐

All these books are available at your local bookshop or newsagent, or can be ordered direct from the publisher. Just tick the titles you want and fill in the form below.

Name ....

Address ....

....

Write to Granada Cash Sales, PO Box 11, Falmouth, Cornwall TR10 9EN.
Please enclose remittance to the value of the cover price plus:
UK: 30p for the first book, 15p for the second book plus 12p per copy for each additional book ordered to a maximum charge of £1.29.
BFPO and EIRE: 30p for the first book, 15p for the second book plus 12p per copy for the next 7 books, thereafter 6p per book.
OVERSEAS: 50p for the first book and 15p for each additional book.
Granada Publishing reserve the right to show new retail prices on covers, which may differ from those previously advertised in the text or elsewhere.